1. DEAL WITH THE TRAUMA

The transformation of the Brussels World Trade Center (WTC) is the first large-scale project dealing with the late modernist heritage of the Northern Quarter and the first step toward giving the neighborhood a new lease on life. An acknowledgment of the value of what is there, keeping in mind the trauma it caused by wiping out a whole part of the city to make way for a 'new' Brussels in the 1970s. The wave of protest triggered by the brutal reshaping some decades ago still resonates today. This made it necessary to approach the transformation of the towers with caution, learning from the lessons of the past.

Befimmo, the owners of the tower and developers of the new project, decided not to leave everything behind and look forward in the usual way, but to look differently. A conscious way of dealing with a complex urban situation and its troubled past, and a shift in posture that takes into account the urban beyond the architectural, in a collective way, by building a conversation with their competitors, the municipality, the architects, urban planners, and a growing group of users and citizens.

01 The World Trade Center was the first fragment of a broader project of segregation locating car traffic on the street level while pedestrian circulation was to be organized on a network of elevated platforms and footbridges. However, this separation never materialized. The spaces on the third floor designed to become public remained inaccessible, while the street level became the main entrance of the building, even though it was initially designed as an infrastructural space to be seen and used only by cars. This unintended and confusing experience of the tower's plinth long overshadowed some of the building's otherwise generous, high-quality spaces.

KEY DATES	ACTORS	KEY STEPS
1947		Shift of the Brussels-North station from Rogier to its current location.
1958		Infrastructual works for the small ring isolate the Northern Quarter from the rest of the city.
1959		First plan to extend the Boulevard Jacquemain to the Northern Quarter.
1962	Groupe Structures	First preliminary drawings of the Manhattan Plan, which aims to transform 20 ha of the Northern Quarter into a new business district.
1964		New road plan for Brussels sets the basis for the Manhattan Plan and the WTC towers.
17/02/1967	Belgian National Government	Official approval of the Manhattan Plan for a new business district in the Northern Quarter or 53 ha of existing city fabric.
1968	Charly De Pauw	First expropriations linked to the Manhattan Plan and Charly De Pauw vision for the WTC.
1970		Start of the construction of WTC I.
1973		Completion of the WTC I tower.
1977		Charly De Pauw is obliged to find foreign capital to continue the construction of the WTC towers.
1977		Completion of the WTC II tower.
1978		End of the expropriations. 53 ha were demolished and 11,000 inhabitants evicted.
1983		Completion of the WTC III tower with foreign (English) capital.
2009		Inauguration of the Zenith tower, last building of the Manhattan Plan. A total of 1.2 million m² of offices are occupied by the public sector.
2015	Befimmo	Launch of an international architecture competition for the future of WTC I to IV.
2015		Befimmo reconsider preservation and approach a specialist in C2C to consult them on sustainability.
2016	Up4North	Foundation of association Up4North by the main real-estate owners of the Northern Quarter (including Befimmo) to promote and rethink the district.
2017	Befimmo	Launch of a competition in association with the BMA (Brussels government architect) to replace WTC I & II.

METROPOLITAN 'OPTIMISM'

In 1958, Brussels hosted the first major World's Fair since World War II. That same year, the decision was taken to establish the European institutions in the city, triggering a lasting surge in business optimism and international metropolitan ambition in the Belgian capital.

It is in this context that in 1967 a group of developers proposed a master plan called the 'Manhattan Plan' for the City of Brussels: a business district made up of towers and urban motorways meant to replace an existing, diverse, and mainly residential neighborhood built in the nineteenth century. While the nearby historical center of Brussels was becoming enshrined and celebrated for its picturesque heritage and touristic potential, its immediate periphery was being sacrificed for the sake of dubious dreams of modern New York grandeur.

One of the Manhattan Plan's crown jewels was the World Trade Center, an ambitious eight-tower complex to be built by developer Charly De Pauw at the intersection of the Northern Quarter's two main roads, now called Boulevard du Roi Albert II and Boulevard Simon Bolivar. The first phase of the project was finished in 1973, inaugurating a first complex of two towers (WTC I and II) located on the northwest corner of the intersection. Offering 110,000 m² of offices, retail space, and underground car parks, the design by architecture office Groupe Structures wrapped the twin buildings in dark Miesian curtain walls and rested them on a hermetic plinth containing a shopping mall.

In the late 1970s, as Charly De Pauw needed additional capital to build the next towers, Japanese investors joined the project. This made it possible to build a second plinth, occupying the southwest corner, as well as one of the two towers topping it (WTC III). To this day, however, the ambitious master plan remains unfinished, while the Manhattan Plan as a whole encountered a similar fate and was never fully realized. Following the early projects from the 1970s, the oil crisis, and the global economic slowdown that delayed completion of the plan, a second pragmatic phase started, aimed at 'filling up' the voids of the Northern Quarter with generic and unimaginative buildings.

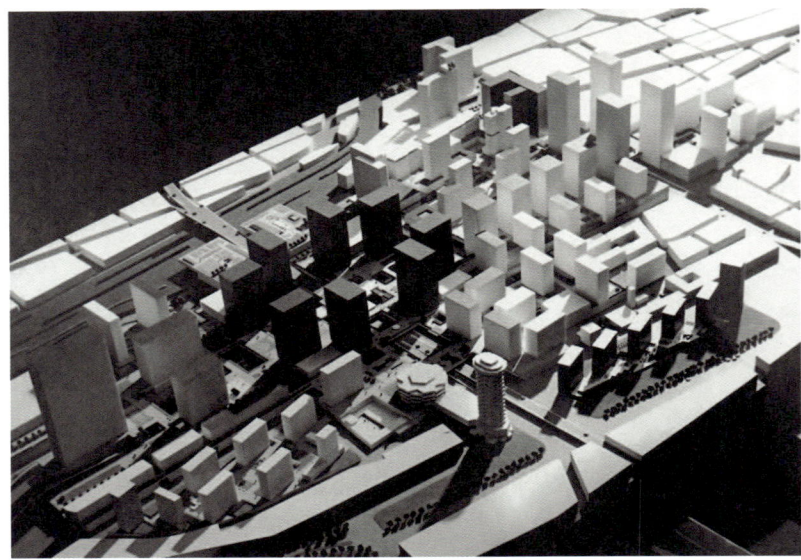

02　Model of the Manhattan Plan. Its uncanny resemblance to a motherboard is no coincidence: like a computer, the dense district was imagined as a tool to efficiently process information and facilitate global trade.

03　The WTC was the symbol of a dream wanting to be reality: world capitalism as herald of progress and welfare, bringing nations together in an international alliance.

04　The Northern Quarter was imagined as a project lifting up the public domain to turn the street level into a purely infrastructural layer providing access—an efficient urban highway that would connect the business district to other cities and financial centers in Europe.

05　Charly De Pauw was the cliché of the Brussels developer: big gestures, big dreams, and close yet questionable connections to key politicians and decision-makers. With his real-estate development company Compagnie de Promotion (CDP), he was at the origins of the Manhattan Plan and the WTC towers. Even though his grand vision for the Northern Quarter was never fulfilled, he made considerable profit with the development of parking garages throughout Belgium.

06   The World Trade Center, depicted here as
      a network of globally connected developments,
      was as much a real-estate asset as a symbol.

07   The one thing that the Manhattan Plan achieved with great success was the eviction of the Northern
      Quarter's inhabitants and the demolition of the existing neighborhood. More than 10,000 people
      were forced to leave their homes, often before the necessary orders were signed. This opportunistic
      attitude, tacitly supported by lenient politicians and administrators, allowed many such projects to
      happen in the city, supporting what became known as 'Brusselization.'

08   The first levels of the WTC were envisioned as dedicated purely to cars
      to provide easy and fast access to the towers. The calmer and brighter
      public spaces were projected on the third floor. Some of these were
      built, but the connections between buildings were never realized.

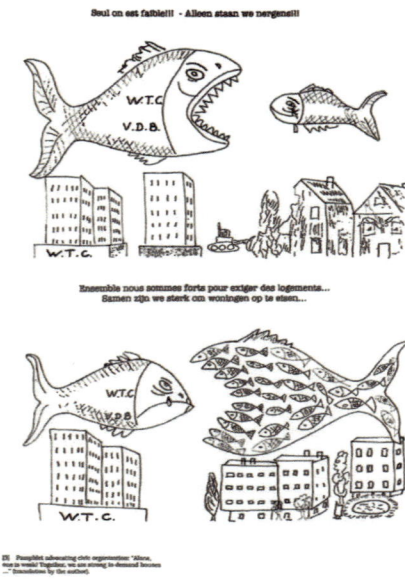

9 In the official discourse built around the project, the existing neighborhood was presented as a 'slum,' rhetorically paving the way for the new project. But the main frustration arose from the fact that most of the relocations promised to inhabitants never happened.

10 In 1975, sociologist Albert Martens released the first of a series of publications detailing the expulsions from the Northern Quarter: *'Rénovation' du quartier de la gare du Nord dans la Région de Bruxelles-Capitale, ou, Le projet Manhattan, World Trade Center et c°: Une libération du sol pour cause d'utilité publique ?*

11 Rather than the developer, a prominent politician of the time was targeted by this drawing: 'VDB,' or Paul Vanden Boeynants.

12 Enthusiasm for a new scale and a new type of city was enhanced in Brussels in the period leading up to Expo 58, the World's Fair. The Northern Quarter was envisioned as a hub connected to a highway network linking Amsterdam to Paris and London to Istanbul. Existing city fabric was hurriedly torn down and replaced with new development, often without much architectural ambition. Plots were regrouped or erased, building heights renegotiated at will, and large-scale car infrastructure deployed all the way into the historical city center.

RESISTANCE

The Manhattan Plan, which was approved by the City of Brussels and the federal government, led to a first series of expropriations in 1968. Over the course of ten years, 11,000 inhabitants were driven out as the buildings that embodied the neighborhood's identity and stability were razed. The demolition of the pre-existing Northern Quarter was a traumatic event for the city at large, and dubbed a 'holocaust' by the area's inhabitants. A tabula rasa opening up the possibility of an artificial kind of greenfield development but which, like many other similar projects happening in postwar Brussels, brought an exceptional level of self-inflicted demolition to the city: a painful process of modernization dubbed 'bruxellisation' (Brusselization).

After the completion of the first two towers of the WTC, the operation appeared to not be as successful as expected, and the Brussels authorities had to organize a 'rescue mission' by renting large portions of the complex for their administrations. The trauma of Brusselization only grew more profound after it became clear that this landmark operation in the Northern Quarter, with the countless demolitions and evictions it had entailed, had only yielded a new administrative center.

In the Northern Quarter, the economic downturns of the 1970s that slowed the project left the neighborhood looking like an uncanny meadow for decades, making the whole ambition of a new business district appear all the more arbitrary and absurd. The plan was also never realized in full: it was supposed to provide more than 5,000 new housing units to rehouse the displaced inhabitants, but by the early 1990s less than half had been built, and the people from the Northern Quarter were long gone.

However, in the late 1960s a grassroots resistance movement against Brusselization started and inhabitant revolt was successful in halting some urban projects, like the demolition of the Marolles, a working-class neighborhood close to the Brussels-South station, which was meant to undergo the same fate as the Northern Quarter. The citizen-driven association ARAU (Atelier de Recherche et d'Action Urbaines, or Workshop for Urban Research and Action) was instrumental in formulating concerns and opposition to modernization projects of debatable quality. They put forward counterproposals taking the interests of inhabitants into account and managed to halt some projects, thus revealing the capacity of the population to weigh in on urban decision-making.

13 The neighborhood after 41 urban blocks had been demolished. Some of the party walls left exposed were used to create a large mural, like an oversized banner, to denounce the project and its impact on the area.

14 The redevelopment of the Northern Quarter triggered significant reactions from the city's inhabitants. In response to the blunt approach to urban planning, civil society began to organize a countermovement, as illustrated in this mural.

15 In reaction to the planned expropriations and expulsions of thousands of residents, protests arose throughout Brussels. Ultimately over 11,000 inhabitants were forced to leave and more than 53 hectares of city fabric were destroyed.

16 The ruthless wave of Brusselization gave rise to a series of counterproposals, the 'contre-projets.' Activist-architects condemned the developments and provided a precise vision of the way they imagined the reconstruction: respect for the urban block, attention to street life, and a readable, classical architecture creating shared civic values. Through this engaged energy, Brussels became one of the test sites for postmodern architecture and urbanism.

NEW HERITAGE

Hostility toward the Northern Quarter remains anchored in the Brussels population to this day. Yet, as a growing number of buildings like the WTC becomes obsolete, the question arises as to the future of late modernism. What is to be done with this heritage that is not 'heritage'? Should this embodiment of postwar business optimism in architecture and urban planning be erased, just like it erased the 'obsolete' urban substance that stood there before it? Should the loop be looped?

Real-estate development company Befimmo, which owned one of the towers, believed in the potential of the WTC and Northern Quarter and decided to acquire the rest of the complex to transform it. In 2015 they launched a first competition calling for a reflection on a 'new' future for the WTC. Almost all participants recommended tearing down the building and rebuilding it from scratch, perpetuating the business as usual of real-estate 'products' reaching the end of their life cycle. The design proposals, formulated by several prominent offices, suggested a kind of modernist reboot: more is more, denser, higher, only this time wrapped in organic forms, greenery, and sustainability. But the developers felt that this was too much, a model no one wanted any longer, and that a new approach was called for.

The transformation of the WTC thus became a testing ground for a reflection on 'how to not demolish a building,' how to deal with the complexity of things and to regard such built substance as a common resource to be valued. An exercise in accepting the 'ugly,' failed, unloved 1960s dream and its dirty 2010s reality, in an attempt to find a position of acknowledgment and remediation.

17–18 As the connection with the other towers never occurred, the shopping center installed on the first and second floors eventually became a place serving only the two WTC towers and catering to the civil servants working there.

19 It was only in the late 1980s that the Northern Quarter underwent a second wave of development that turned it into an administrative district. This later phase of development was heavily influenced by the contre-projet movement and aesthetic. Yet, while part of the new projects was indeed mixed developments, the buildings erected along the main axis changed appearance but not content. Boulevard du Roi Albert II thus became a monofunctional strip, looking like a kind of airport business park. At the center of the aerial picture found in the corridors of the WTC complex in 2017, a complete set of eight World Trade Center towers is visible. A photomontage prolonging the fantasy.

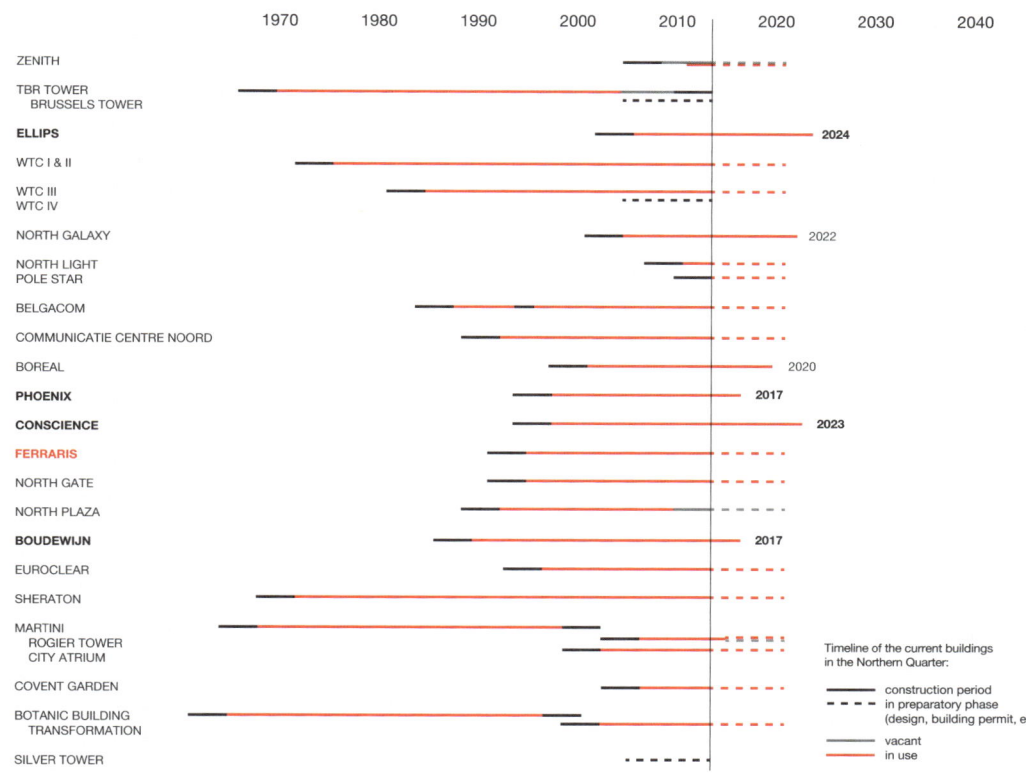

21 In 2017 and 2018, a visit to the roof of WTC I was often the first experience Befimmo offered stakeholders. This emphasized both the panoramic potential of the rooftop and the strategic location of the building within Brussels.

20 For their study on the redevelopment of the Ferraris office building, Bogdan & Van Broeck and IDEA Consult made an overview of the realization, lease, and vacancy of office buildings in the Brussels Northern Quarter. It visualizes how many leases were ending or spaces becoming vacant in the 2010s.

Timeline of the current buildings in the Northern Quarter:
— construction period
- - - in preparatory phase (design, building permit, etc.)
— vacant
— in use

22 As the owner of WTC III and parts of WTC I and II, Befimmo launched a twofold process. On the one hand, they gradually acquired full ownership of WTC I and II, creating conditions allowing for a complete transformation of the towers. On the other hand, they invited five international teams of architects for a competition addressing all four WTC towers at once (including WTC IV, which was never built). A way to imagine a new life for the towers while effectively linking back to the initial international ambitions of the Manhattan Plan.

A SHIFT IN POSTURE

Befimmo realized that they couldn't change the WTC without changing the neighborhood, which as a whole was suffering from a lack of appeal and a high vacancy rate. This could only be achieved collectively, and in 2016, on Befimmo's initiative, Up4North was created. This alliance of Northern Quarter property owners (also including AG Real Estate, Allianz Benelux, AXA Belgium, Banimmo, Belfius Insurance, Immobel, and Triuva) scaled up the architectural question of the towers to an urban question touching the whole district.

The initial intention to change the image of the Northern Quarter and improve its appeal was broadened to include an attempt to understand the neighborhood in all its complexity and to articulate the global dynamics of the real-estate sector (such as more volatile rental markets, shorter leases, shrinking need for office space) with the local reality of inhabitants and civil society—both a pragmatic reaction to a changing market in which sustainability and social responsibility can no longer be ignored and a genuine attempt at opening up and venturing into unknown territory.

Befimmo then launched a second competition concerning the WTC, this time in association with the Brussels Bouwmeester (government architect), to select a design team in charge of developing a new scheme for the transformation of the towers. This more collaborative approach followed the company's Corporate Social Responsibility program, looking beyond mere financial value, following the Sustainable Development Goals formulated by the United Nations in 2015. Through the project, the idea grew within Befimmo that they could do more: a shift from the 1970s brashness embodied by Charly De Pauw and from an unwavering belief in 'the new.'

23–24 As part of their redevelopment strategy, Befimmo and other property owners of the neighborhood launched the initiative Up4North, a platform to open up a debate and gather insights through a series of workshops and roundtable discussions gathering diverse stakeholders. A modest initiative, yet one striving to reflect on the future of the neighborhood in the absence of a policy framework.

2018: Strategic axes

These various points of view enabled us to make the strategy evolve and define our priorities in six areas that reflect the way we view our business today and tomorrow.

- **Integration into the city:** the building becomes an ecosystem open to its urban environment that brings together a mix of functions;
- **The world of work:** rethinking workspaces based on the type of activity and profile of the users;
- **Setting an example:** Befimmo shares the benefit of its research with all its partners and uses its influence to foster positive developments in society;
- **Mobility:** contributing to the development of alternative, environmentally-friendly transport solutions;
- **Dialogue:** fostering and maintaining communication with all its stakeholders;
- **Use of resources:** applying the principles of eco-design and the circular economy at each phase of a building's life cycle.

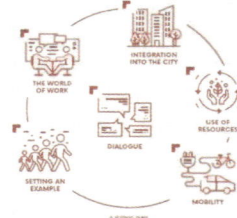

Besides these 6 strategic axes, other priorities like CSR governance, ethics, compliance and recognitions are also put forward.

Although many initiatives have already emerged on each of these topics, Befimmo intends to innovate further by adopting a participatory approach with its team. All staff were invited to share their thoughts on these topics and to register for one or more of them, according to their inclinations. The objective is to continue debating them with a view to taking other concrete initiatives and projects to develop each area and associate them with objectives.

The strategy is part of an innovation strategy aimed at integrating social responsibility into the core of the Company's everyday activities and translating it into sustainable development opportunities for all.

For Befimmo SA

Benoît De Blieck
Managing Director

Alain Devos
Chairman of the Board

2

25   As a real-estate company listed on the stock market, Befimmo formulated a Corporate Social Responsibility program based on financial, social, and ecological values that directly influenced their approach to the transformation of the WTC.

2. CONFRONT AND LEARN

Inspired by the artist collective that was already using the 25th floor of the WTC I tower for ateliers and meeting spaces, in February 2017 51N4E organized a students' workshop on the 19th floor, investigating the notion of reusing '70s monofunctional office buildings as a way to create Hybrid Business Districts. The idea of hybrid occupation was tested both by being on-site in the WTC and by looking at the case study of the nearby CCN building. The experience —facilitated by the recently created Up4North— inspired a project for temporary use, testing to expand the use of the tower for smaller and more diverse organizations.

The temporary use became a reality in the WTC and was accompanied by many events enabling exchanges to take place on-site, in the very towers that would soon be transformed. During this period, the tower was inhabited in many ways, accommodating working, teaching, student parties, Wednesday play for families with young children, launch events for political initiatives, and a rooftop garden, to name just a few. As part of the temporary use, a project atelier was also set up in the tower, allowing the team reflecting on its transformation to work together on the future of the building.

A multiform learning environment was generated by the many trajectories intersecting in the WTC—trajectories that were not centrally coordinated, that did not articulate a formalized participation scheme, and that sometimes questioned or contradicted each other. These trajectories of learning all took place within and around the building, creating confrontations as opportunities for a fertile discussion on the Northern Quarter and its challenges, all directly informing the transformation project of the tower.

KEY DATES	ACTORS	KEY STEPS
2015	Artist collective coordinated by Overtoon	Short-term lease of the 25th floor
06–17/02/2017	51N4E, UHasselt	On-site master class Hybrid Business District
26/06/2017– 02/09/2017	Real Estate Architecture	Real Estate Architecture summer school
	KU Leuven	Temporary occupation
August 2017	51N4E, Vraiment Vraiment	Moving in on-site with the entire office on the 16th floor
September 2017	51N4E, Up4North, Architecture Workroom Brussels, Vraiment Vraiment	Creating a de facto alliance to coordinate the activation of the towers (and the district)
October 2017	KU Leuven Sint-Lucas Brussels Campus	Setting up of design studio spaces for the academic year 2017–18 on the 24th floor
November 2017	LabNorth	Open call for temporary use for starters, small organizations, and associations
December 2017	Architecture Workroom Brussels	Moving in on the 16th floor
January 2018	Diverse non-profits and designers, local radio station, Samenlevingsopbouw Brussel, Nansen, Service Volontaire International, etc.	Moving in on the 17th to the 26th floors
02/06/2018 – 08/07/2018	AWB, IABR	*You Are Here* (Part One)
June 2018	LabNorth	Urban roof garden
22/06/2018	Onkruid	Creative Shaping Cities
15/09/2018 – 11/11/2018	AWB, IABR	*You Are Here* (Part Two)
11–14/10/2018	Brasserie Illegaal	Illegaal Festivaal

26   Concept sketch by Freek Persyn (51N4E) illustrating the temporary activation of WTC I.

WORKSHOP WTC

In 2017 a workshop was organized by 51N4E in collaboration with the architecture department of Hasselt University (UHasselt). The aim was to reflect on adaptive reuse for modernist office structures and on possible ways the Northern Quarter could transition out of its monofunctional nature to include new uses and users. It took as a case study the Centre de Communication Nord (CCN), an office building situated on top of the Brussels-North station.

The studio was installed for a week on the 19th floor of WTC I, which by then was largely vacant. It tackled multiple levels, consulting and debating with different stakeholders, before concluding with two ideas to test this possible hybridity: on the one hand, an affordable temporary occupation format with an 'in return' policy, and on the other hand, a 'project of projects' made of small-scale interventions distributed in space and time.

This workshop—a pioneering spatial situation in itself—was followed by a presentation of its findings to the board of Befimmo and Up4North. This was the beginning of an exchange, making it possible to connect with many different levels and people at once. In the wake of the workshop, further discussions took place, during which the idea of a temporary occupation of the WTC grew.

27   Poster announcing the Hybrid Business Districts workshop, February 2017.

28   On-site studio of the Hybrid Business Districts workshop, organized by 51N4E in the framework of the Adaptive Reuse master program of the UHasselt architecture school.

29   Government architect Kristiaan Borret and Frederik Serroen looking out from WTC I during a presentation by master's students of the UHasselt architecture school.

30 Presentation of an extensive urban scale model of the Northern Quarter on a vacant floor of WTC I.

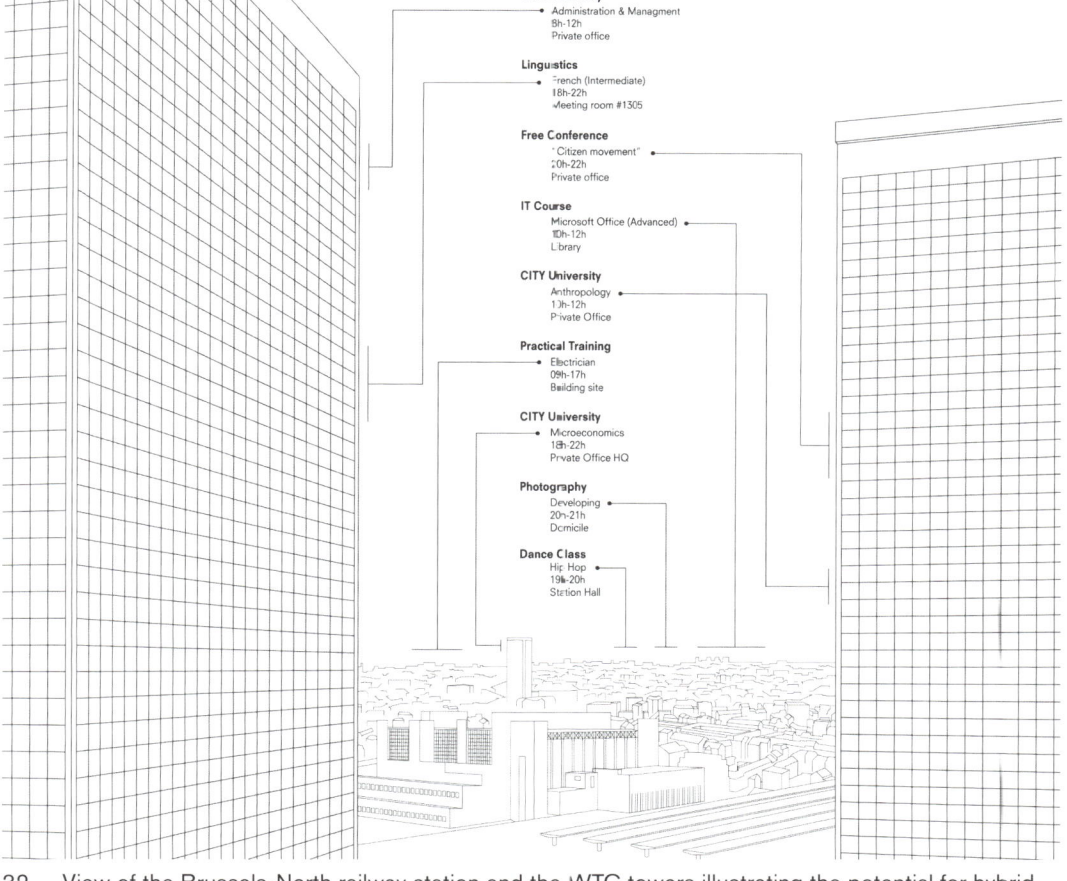

31 Inspired by the initial workshop in February, the KU Leuven Sint-Lucas Brussels Campus took the bold step to occupy the whole 24th floor from September 2017 on and turn it into an atelier for multiple design studios.

32 View of the Brussels-North railway station and the WTC towers illustrating the potential for hybrid occupation, produced by 51N4E and l'AUC in 2011 as part of the Brussels 2040 urban study.

PRE-OCCUPATION

The vacancy of the WTC, which was the starting point of the whole reflection, resulted from several factors: its monofunctional character and lack of appeal in spite of its excellent location; its outdated offer of office space lacking flexibility in the contemporary digital context; its unsustainability (a contemporary no-go for many companies trying to obtain green certifications); and finally the high rents of the Northern Quarter, which led many businesses to relocate to other, less expensive parts of the city following the 2008 economic crisis.

One of the aims of the temporary occupation scheme was to test a transition from big long-term tenants to a mix enabling smaller tenants or even individuals to rent office spaces too. A platform called LabNorth was created, providing an inventory of the vacant spaces of the Northern Quarter available for rent at a very low price, as long as the occupant committed to offering something in return to the other users of the building or to the neighborhood (by organizing talks, exhibitions, screenings, launches, classes, or providing various services). In 2017 the temporary and multi-tenant occupation of WTC I by a diverse group of users started, with nonprofits, architecture offices, artists, the KU Leuven Sint-Lucas Brussels Campus architecture school, and cultural organizations moving in. 51N4E tested this model firsthand, sharing the 16th floor with Architecture Workroom Brussels, including communal facilities such as large meeting rooms, a kitchen, a greenhouse, a model workshop.

The temporary occupation made it possible to experience the unexpected beauty of the building, the qualities of the place, the view, the location, and all the uses that could potentially function there beyond corporate offices. Over the one-year period, the Hybrid Business District was tested in situ and in actu: a 'pre-occupation' whose many trials ultimately permeated the WTC's transformation project.

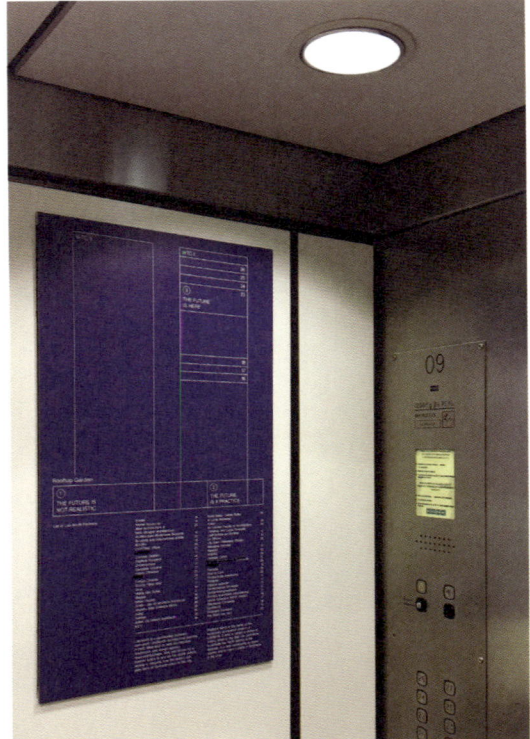

33 Wayfinding panel of the temporary use: the only moment that the scope of the operation became legible as a whole. Some of the artists on the 25th floor didn't consider themselves part of the temporary use and consequently covered up their names.

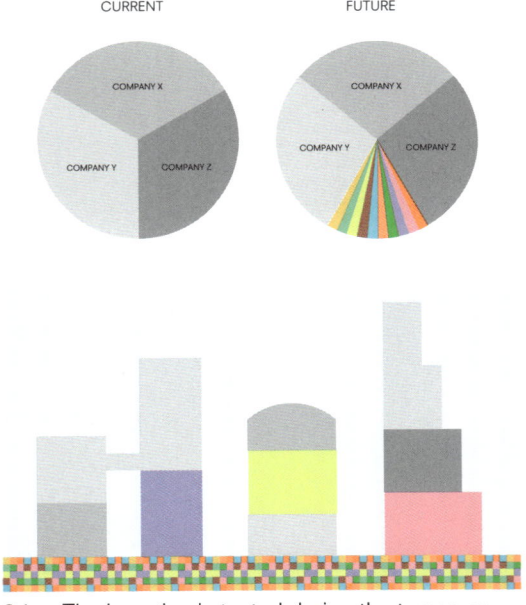

CURRENT   FUTURE

34 The hypothesis tested during the temporary occupation of WTC I was a multi-tenant model in which a diversity of organizations rent and share spaces. This type of occupation departed radically from the area's former single-tenant model.

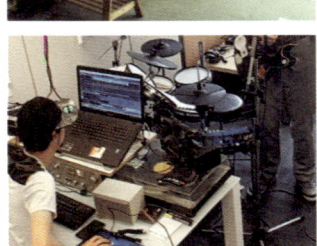

35 The many organizations renting spaces in the framework of Platform North, posing in their workspaces. Documented by Vraiment Vraiment.

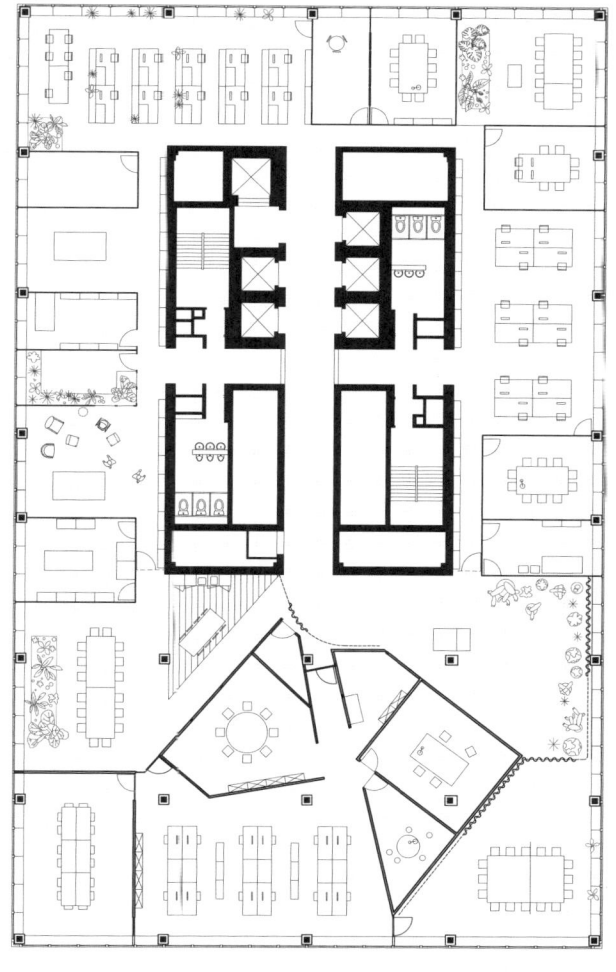

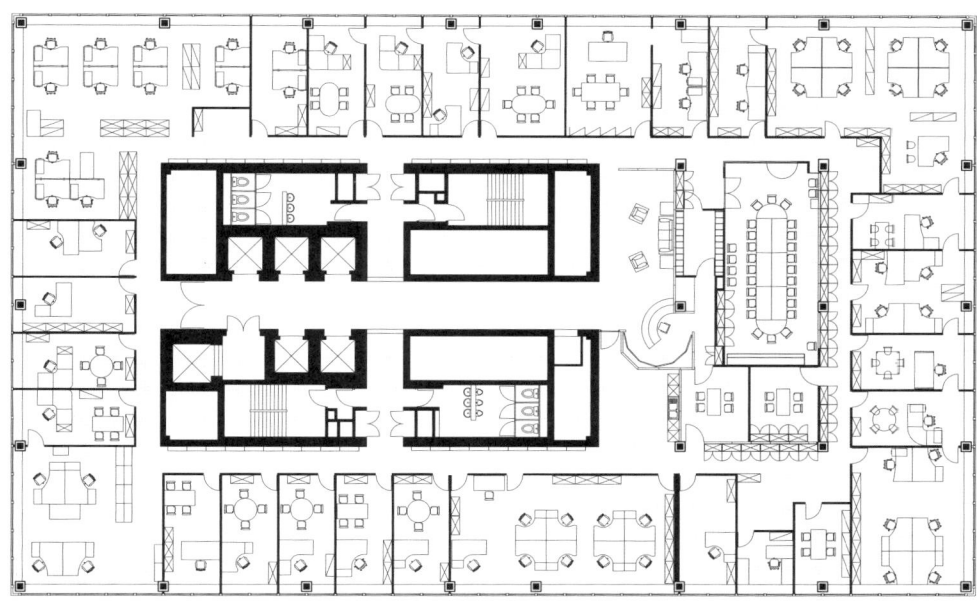

36   Plan of the 16th floor of WTC I (above right), where architecture office 51N4E, 'think-and-do-tank' Architecture Workroom Brussels, and communication agency Vraiment Vraiment collectively ran LabNorth while sharing spaces and facilities. The WTC II tower (below left) was then still in use by the administration.

The temporary occupation functioned as a test site, making it possible to try out different ways of using the building and different spatial atmospheres, but also to connect to a broader cultural and citizen network, expanding the occupation with a variety of events.

An important parallel program was the roof garden installed on top of the towers' plinth, for which a specific call was launched that was aimed at users interested in being part of a project of urban cultivation. It was handled by some of the temporary office tenants as well as by inhabitants from the neighborhood.

37   During the opening of *You Are Here*, the collective Pool Is Cool and the design practice Alive Architecture joined forces to transform the fountain on the roundabout next to the towers into a swimming pool.

38   On weekdays after school and on weekends, a group of families with small kids came to the roof garden to hang out and play in a self-constructed tower.

39   A pool party that lasted for a day, complete with inflatable toys, lounge chairs, and a beach bar. A local school came by to play in the temporary pool during their recess.

2. Confront and Learn

How to Not Demolish a Building

40   In the summer of 2018, a call was launched for urban gardening projects to be installed on the socle of the WTC towers. Various people and organizations came together, creating a patchwork of different parcels accommodating vegetables anc flowers.

41   On the 23rd floor of WTC I, one of the existing windows was replaced by one that could open and allow outside air to flow into the space. This window test was both a mock-up for the new project and part of the exhibition *You Are Here.*

42   Rucola, basil, tomatoes, and other small vegetables grew in the rooftop garden and participants took turns watering them.

43   In the former bank space on the first floor, a replica of the storefront of Recyclart, a grassroots cultural center that had recently lost its premises in Brussels's city center, was installed.

You Are Here, the International Architecture Biennale Rotterdam (IABR), was a culmination of all the tracks that were started at the beginning of the temporary occupation. Held in 2018 and curated by Architecture Workroom Brussels, it turned the towers into the 'World Transformation Center' for several months, drawing a lot of visitors to the building. This included many people who formerly did not have access to these spaces: school kids taking part in activities organized there, practitioners related to the projects shown and discussed by the Biennale, and citizens visiting the exhibition.

The many workshops that were held in the tower on the occasion of the IABR introduced various discussions relevant to the city and the neighborhood, such as mobility transition, the ecological deficit, and the question of social justice in urban transformation. The IABR also triggered a critical response from actors exterior to the tower, who reacted to the ongoing transformation project and its objectives and public. For instance, the exhibition's slogan 'The Future Is Here' was ironically reformulated on social media as 'Whose Future Is Here?'

44 A youth festival organized by Illegaal, a local brewery and temporary tenant of the building, occupied the base floors of the tower for some time. The levels formerly accommodating retail became party spaces, with shops becoming dance floors and the escalators used as skateboarding ramps.

45 As part of their course on ethics in architecture, Gideon Boie and Lieven Decauter developed a public program of lectures with their students. One of them was titled 'Welcome to Jaspers Town.' It underlined the recurring presence of the architecture firm Jaspers-Eyers in large-scale real-estate developments in Brussels. The poster was hung in the elevators used by the architecture students and teachers who were occupying one of the tower's floors as well as by the architects from Jaspers-Eyers who worked on another floor.

46 Part of the exhibition was a pair of binoculars placed on a platform at the windows of the 23th floor of WTC I, through which you could look at Brussels and the neighborhood.

47 The banner of the *You Are Here* exhibition designed by London-based firm OK-RM, provocatively appealing to the city beyond the circles of usual suspects.

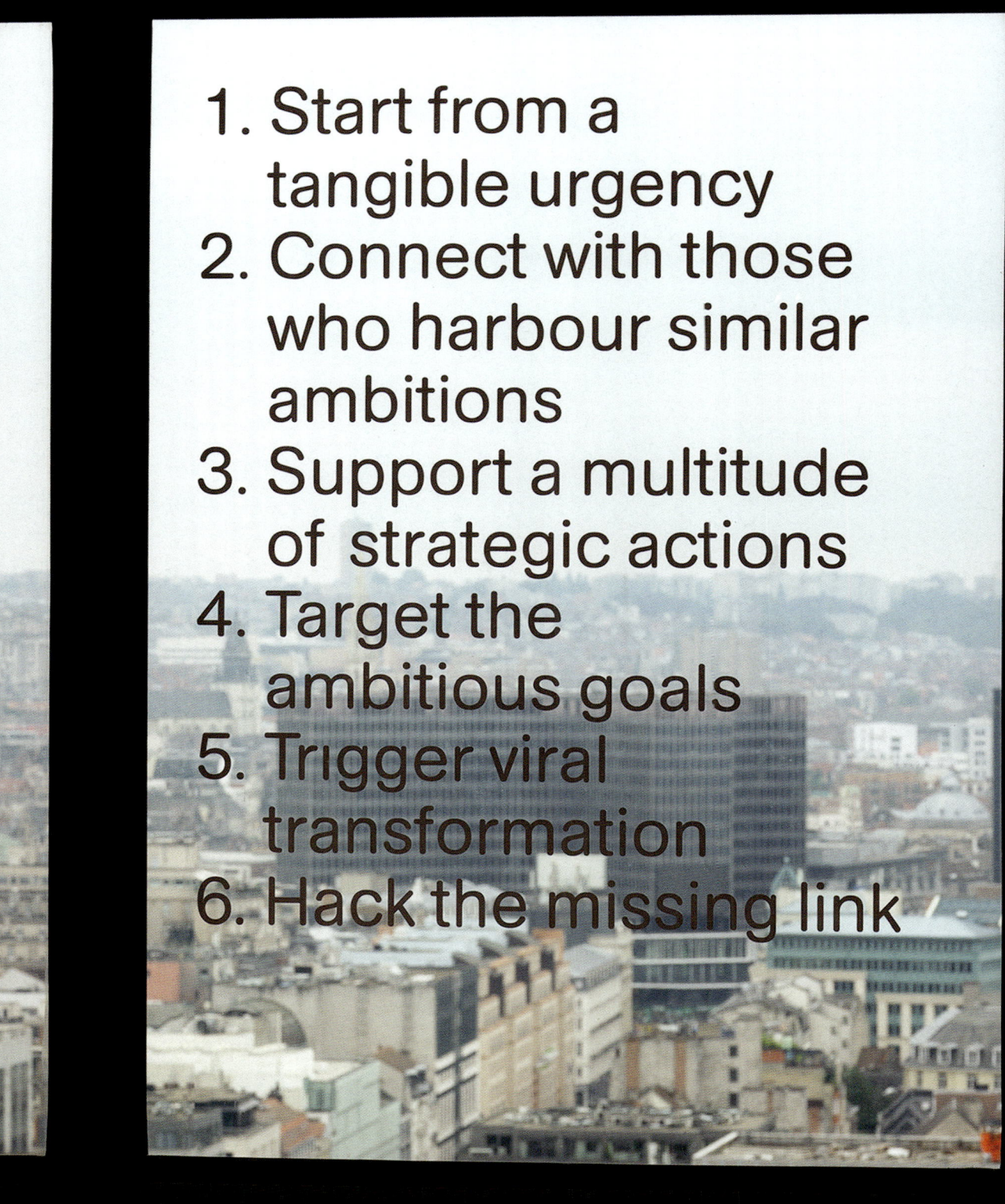

The building is the STAGE
The building is the TEST-SITE
The building is the EXHIBITION

Het gebouw is het PODIUM
Het gebouw is de TEST-SITE
Het gebouw is de TENTOONS

Le bâtiment est le PODIUM
Le bâtiment est le TERRAIN D'
Le bâtiment est L'EXPOSITION

3. START WITH THE STRUCTURE

While planning the transformation of the towers, Befimmo, in a rather unusual move for a private developer, addressed the Brussels Bouwmeester, asking him to help steer the process. He accepted under two conditions: to launch an open call for the selection of the design team and to make the program of the transformed building hybrid by mixing offices with other uses. A way to turn the reflection into a testing ground for strategies that could be expanded to the whole neighborhood.

In September 2017 the call was launched to select a design team to join Jaspers-Eyers Architects, a large firm that already was involved with Befimmo. Architects 51N4E and urban planners l'AUC teamed up to answer the call. They were first shortlisted, and after a short competition procedure they were selected to join the project team. Just before the work started, the Flemish Government launched a tender procedure that it would be looking for offices around the Brussels-North station to move into by 2023.

Following the proposal by 51N4E and l'AUC, Befimmo installed a temporal project atelier on the 15th floor of WTC I. This neutral ground became a shared environment for design and reflection, making it possible to reshape relations and the collaboration between designers and investor. This was an integrated way of working together, and of reflecting on the formulation of a highly adaptable structure.

The proposed design, reusing the existing cores of the WTC, focused on creating new spatial conditions complementing both the floor heights and surfaces of the existing towers. By adding a central slab every second floor connecting both towers, a new, generous scale was introduced for both the building and the neighborhood.

KEY DATES	ACTORS	KEY STEPS
September 2017	Befimmo	Launch of an architecture competition in association with the Brussels Bouwmeester.
September 2017	Flemish Government	Flemish Government launched a tender for a new location for their administration
November 2017	51N4E, l'AUC, Befimmo	Mixed-use project ZIN is selected as winning proposal.
January 2018	51N4E, l'AUC, Jaspers-Eyers	Setup of the project atelier on the 15th floor of WTC I.
June 2018	51N4E, l'AUC, Jaspers-Eyers	Building permit is handed in for the construction of ZIN
July 2018	Befimmo	Application as candidate for the tender of a new location of the offices of the Flemish Government.
March 2019	Flemish Government, Befimmo	Agreement on the selection of ZIN as the future offices for 3,900 employees of the Flemish Government.
March 2020	urban.brussels	Urban and environmental building permits obtain green light.
December 2020	TM Open Minds (CFE – Van Laere – BPC – VMA)	Construction of new foundations for the 'Volume Capable.'

1972 2020 2023

48   The transformation from WTC I and II to ZIN was developed around the existing structure, following the structural grid of the foundations and working with the existing cores.

A NEW SCALE

The transformation of the World Trade Center was approached as a pilot project: a reflection valuing a different kind of heritage and almost a manifesto to prove that, for such structures, adaptive reuse is also a possibility.

Before the open call launched by the Bouwmeester, the architecture firm Jaspers-Eyers had already produced a sketch design for a new building to be used by candidates as a starting point or a basis on which to react. This initial design focused solely on mixing uses, but did not include the question of reuse or hybridity.

Going beyond a mere programmatic diversity, the competition proposal by 51N4E and l'AUC replied to the question for a truly hybrid space for the present as well as the future by giving a spatial and structural answer. The founding design decision of the project was the projection of a central slab—the 'Volume Capable'—a stacking of double-height floors connecting the two towers, 22 m wide, 100 m long, 6.4 m high, without any circulation cores or shafts. An intervention that does not add a lot of square meters, but does add a lot of volume, offering a whole new scale to the neighborhood and departing from the formatted offer that was so detrimental to the area's appeal. Something radically different from what is available today, introducing new possibilities.

The building will accommodate large office surfaces, flats, a hotel, a co-working space, shared facilities like a sports center, and publicly accessible spaces like the greenhouse. Yet the new building was not tailor-made for those specific programs. It was approached as an architecture of conditions and structure rather than one of functions and expression: a space for hybrid use.

49 Competition model of ZIN, during the Flemish Government's public tender, July 2018.

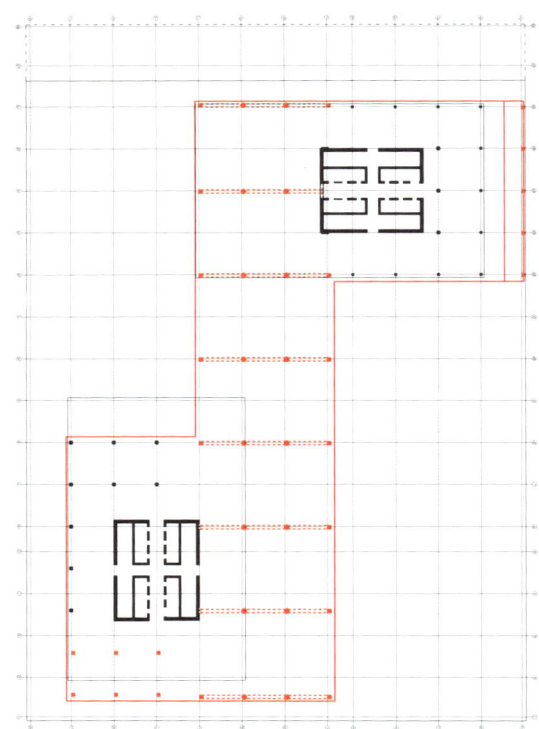

50 Plan showing the existing towers (in black) and the new intervention (in red).

51 Structural diagram by the engineering office Greisch, exploring a scenario increasing the floor height by removing some floor slabs and installing a new floor slab instead. As a result, three floors are reduced to two higher ones. This diagram that explores the height variations in the building inspired the spatial concept of the Volume Capable.

How to Not Demolish a Building

52   Plan showing a full office floor's possible spatial organization. The height of the central part is double that of the other areas.

53   A 1:33 study model of a typical office floor. An interior landscape, meeting spaces as rooms inside a room. The multiplicity of situations and working environments allows for many possible ways to work, meet, and exchange.

54–56 Three 'exceptional' work environments that are possible in the new 'typical' floors due to the scale of the new space. These configurations enable both interactive learning environments and attractive work settings to concentrate, like the forest or the reading room.

57 During the competition phase, the Flemish Government requested to show the actual possibilities for the space planning of their office floors according to the 'New Ways of Working,' which is centered on activity-based workspaces. The starting point of this exercise was a basic organization of the circulation flows and the main shared functions such as lockers, sanitary amenities, and printing rooms, around the two cores (plan below left). Consecutively, multiple space layouts were developed that all offer different sizes of spaces and relationships between them. Ultimately this shows that the offices can range from the classical partitioned office to more dynamic setups with bigger spaces for interaction, and even project-based clusters where teams have their own private part of the floor with a triangular open space and adjacent project rooms.

58 The office environment relies heavily on the natural qualities the architecture allows: giving abundant space, bringing in daylight, offering open views, letting in natural air, installing luscious greenery.

Each of the double-height floors in the Volume Capable also extends with the single-height floors of the towers, offering single 4,500 m^2 plateaus with diverse conditions—something quite exceptional for a high-rise office building—while the floors of the towers that are not connected to the central volume are independent and therefore free to become anything else.

This was dubbed a 'zebra' occupation scheme, making it possible to organize all of the office programs on only 14 floors, lending the building the ease of circulation of a low-rise while still offering the qualities of a high-rise. This scheme initially came about as a way of reacting to the two existing cores, which suddenly had to serve three distinct programs (offices, flats, and a hotel). The zebra was a way to make sure that the cores would only have to serve one program per floor, to avoid having to split them in plan.

This spatial and volumetric reshuffling creates a highly versatile set of spaces that can be freely arranged and rearranged to fit the needs of a tenant, or of successive tenants. A new kind of environment for variegated uses, it offers increased adaptability and durability for the whole building.

With simple decisions like the addition of extra evacuation stairs in the existing cores, the potential for hybridity is further increased: according to current regulations, each floor could host up to 700 people, meaning that the building could easily be converted in the future into a higher occupancy facility, like a public building or a school. A hybridity supported by the design, taking place in space, but also potentially in time.

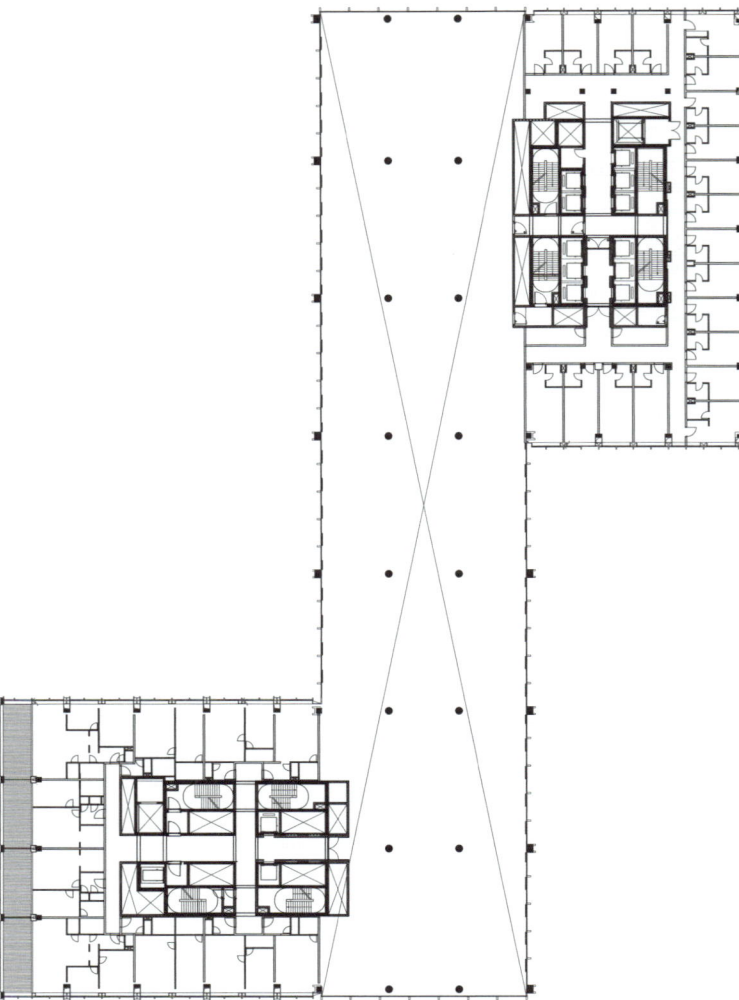

59   The intermediate floors of the building are accommodating other programs: a hotel in the north tower and housing in the south tower.

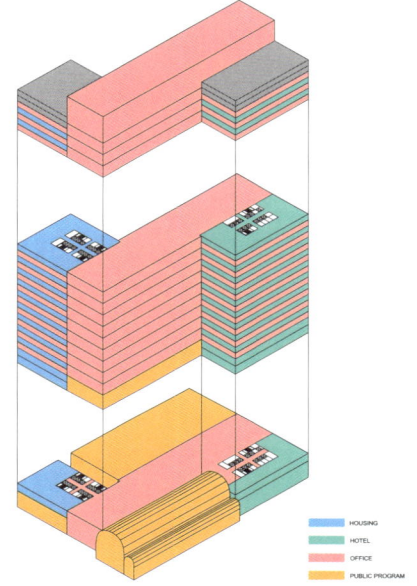

HOUSING
HOTEL
OFFICE
PUBLIC PROGRAM

60   The continuous office floors created between the Volume Capable and the towers will combine different spatial atmospheres, making it possible to adapt to the needs of the future occupants. Each typical floor is a combination of single-height office spaces around the cores and double-height ones in the Volume Capable.

61   Each level features large 'covered terraces.' They become an inhabitable exterior space for both the housing floors (connected to the largest apartments) and the office floors.

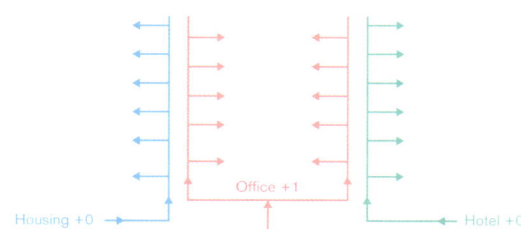

Housing +0   Office +1   Hotel +0

62   The 'zebra' occupation scheme lets the three main programs (offices, housing, and hotel) share two shafts. By raising the entrance of the Flemish Government's offices to the first floor, an alternating pattern of independent access emerges for the three addresses, thus solving this circulation puzzle.

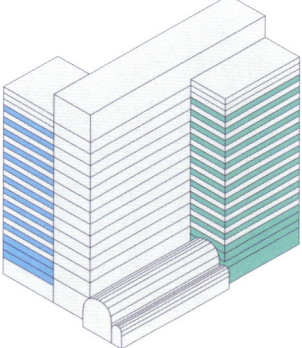

63   The Northern Quarter, having only monofunctional office buildings in its central part, becomes a desolate and unwelcoming place after 5:00 p.m. By inserting apartments and a hotel in the new project, there will be, for the first time, continuous activity on the principal axis of the district, also during the evening. Due to the zebra scheme, this is even spread over the full height, so the entire building is lively 24/7.

A NEUTRAL FRAMEWORK

The radical design of conditions for the building is independent from specific programs. The design team agreed early on that the zebra scheme, although quite exceptional, should not be expressed in the façade to avoid tying the building's expression to a programmatic division that might evolve in the future. Following that logic, the façade doesn't distinguish office floors from flats or hotel floors, presenting a seemingly undifferentiated face to the city. However, the project reacts softly to its surroundings, for instance when it opens itself up to the nearby Maximilian Park with loggias offered both to flats and offices, or to the Brussels-North station with the public greenhouse on the ground floor.

64　Early sketch drawing of the transformed WTC I and II. Five new architectural volumes readdress the building toward the city.

65　Setting during the *You Are Here* exhibition, where the first framework for the renovation of the tower was shown and experienced. A glass panel was taken out of the existing façade and replaced by a sliding window. It made clear that the basic qualities of view, appropriation of the façade, and letting in natural air were clearly shared between offices and apartments. This confirmed the strategy to look for a contextual architectural answer rather than a programmatic one.

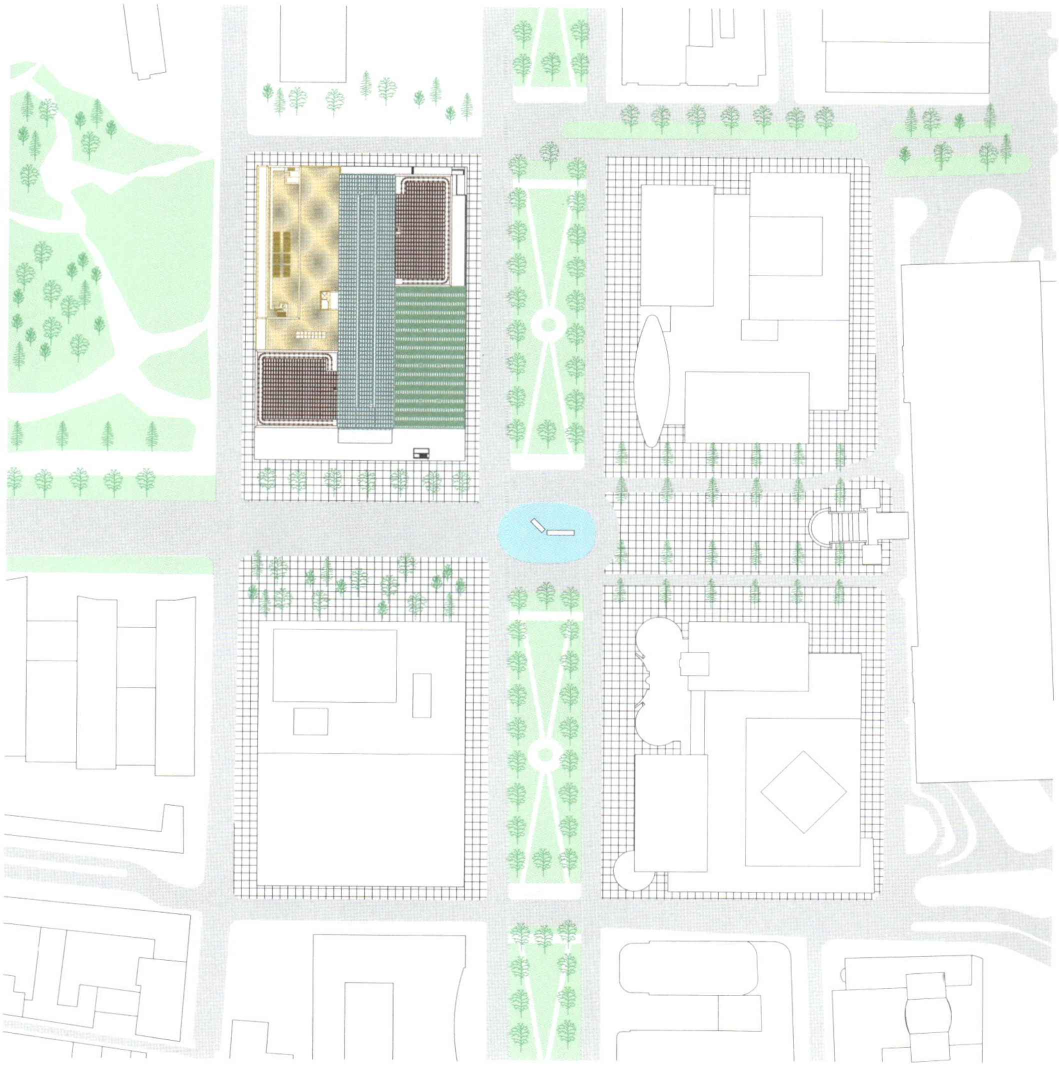

66–67　Diagrams of the four 'architectures': (1) greenhouse, (2) towers, (3) park building, (4) Volume Capable.

NEW WAYS OF INHABITING

The unobstructed plan of the Volume Capable, the height variations, and the vast, unified office floors open up many possibilities of occupation, and those simple parameters of the project ultimately offer the possibility of multiple and varied work environments. A life and quality generated by the building, taking place within its clear and undifferentiated framework, showing the wide-ranging capacity of this new spatial context in the city.

68 The building rendered at dusk, showing the multiple environments that are produced, each relating in its own way to the context and also expressing its individual qualities toward the city.

69 The section shows the main structural adaptations of the original WTC I and II: inserting the new double-height volume, opening up the plinth, and adding terraces on one of the towers.

4. COMMIT TO CIRCULARITY

Since the start of the reflection on the transformation of the World Trade Center in 2017, circularity has been one of the main drivers of the alternative future for the renovation of the towers. After the Flemish Government announced that it would be looking for new offices, Befimmo raised the ambition they originally described in their own competition outline to match the high sustainability of Flemish public buildings: an ecological and sustainable evaluation grid called 'GRO: Towards Future-Oriented Building Projects,' setting a number of targets ranging from the energy efficiency of the building all the way to its life cycle or construction method.

Those requirements opened up a whole thought process in the design team and spurred research on how to design consciously. An alternative mindset, in which all decisions needed to be looked at through a new prism. The conception phase approached circularity as a reflection not only on reuse and material choices, but also on reversibility and the design of spaces capable of handling change to become as durable as possible.

Everyone committed to a quest for an overall responsible environment, and a process of trial and error, of learning, in which all participants found themselves in the position of a beginner, reflecting on this recent built heritage with different eyes while trying out possible interventions using mock-ups directly on-site.

KEY DATES	ACTORS	KEY STEPS
26/01/2018		Visit to Venlo City Hall, the first circular public building of the Low Countries.
March 2018	Lateral Thinking Factory	Brainstorm sessions on a circular building.
March 2018	Flemish Government	Introduction to GRO, an integrative durability tool of the Flemish Government.
April 2018	OVAM, Leefmilieu Brussel, Service Public de Wallonie	Launch of TOTEM (Tool to Optimise the Total Environmental impact of Materials). ZIN is used as a test case.
03/06/2018	Drees & Sommer	Inventarization of the whole building.
March – December 2019	Rotor, De Meuter, Drees & Sommer	Search for buyers, organising the collect and dismantling of building elements to be reused off-site.
July 2020 – Spring 2023	De Meuter, Drees & Sommer, ShipIt, Travie	Packing of concrete tiles from the rooftop of WTC I & II and transport to nearby storage facility for re-use in ZIN.
June 2019 – March 2020	51N4E, Dzero Studio	Research on reuse of interior façade cover panels from WTC in ZIN.
15/01/2020	urban.brussels	ZIN is awarded with a BE.Exemplary award by the Brussels-Capital Region.
08/12/2020	De Meuter	Dismantling of the main structure of the towers and plinth.
11/06/2021	CCB, Ergon, Prefaco	First concrete with C2C Silver certification is poured on-site.

70   The original foundations, underground floors, and two cores aboveground are kept (in gray). This represented more than 60 per cent of the original mass of the WTC I and II buildings.

71   Mock-up of a coffered ceiling system made of plasterboard to finish the existing steel skeleton of the WTC towers. A strategy to generate the most generous possible ceiling height while also providing the required fire-resistant, acoustic, and thermal properties to the floor slabs. A mock-up of a living room was later installed to test the kind of living space such a solution would foster.

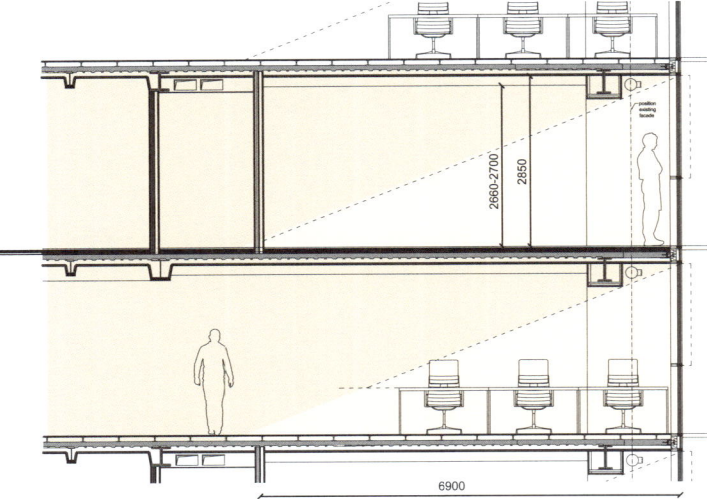

72   Section drawn at the same stage of the project, showing a one-meter offset of the original façade, allowing the integration of vertical ventilation shafts in front of the structural columns. This was a way to prevent ventilation ducts from having to cross from core to façade, which would have made it necessary to lower the ceiling height. Although formulated during an initial reflection on total reuse, this specific solution nevertheless made it into the final project.

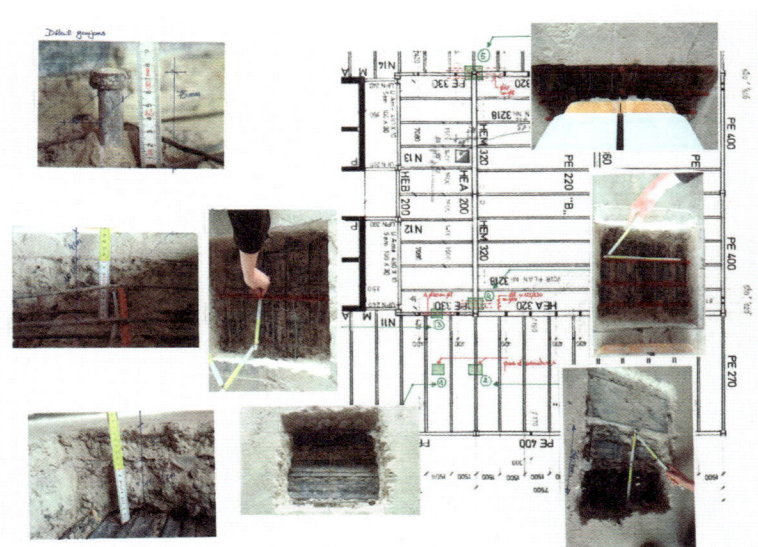

73   Destructive investigation performed by the structural engineer. One of the many steps of a study phase leading to the conclusion that the floor slabs could not be kept, mostly because they were structurally unable to transfer the loads coming from the new Volume Capable.

CIRCULAR AMBITIONS

The sustainability standards demanded by the Flemish Government—and the focus they place on circular construction—deeply influenced the architectural response to the competition for the reuse of the towers. It gave a big advantage to the conservation of a majority of the building's substance, although the uncertainty of working with the existing structure made the project more unpredictable.

Engineers had to carry out a kind of archaeology of the structure to assess the possibility of keeping various components. In parallel, the project team made investigations and formulated design scenarios to think of ways of inhabiting the existing floors, for instance by replacing windows with openable ones or treating added fire protection architecturally with ceiling cassettes.

However, it gradually appeared that the steel skeleton and floor slabs could not be retained. Beyond difficulties with fire and acoustic regulations, the slabs of the towers had moved unevenly over the years, and connecting them with the new slabs of the Volume Capable was impossible without a considerable loss in floor height. Similarly, the existing floor slabs were too weak to transfer the wind loads of the new central volume.

A hybrid strategy was chosen that proved more financially feasible than complete reuse. It combines partial demolition (leading to material repurposing and recycling) with the preservation of the existing cores, underground levels, and foundations, and the construction of a new plinth, new towers around the existing cores, and the Volume Capable connecting both towers.

With less ambitious demands from the potential tenant of the offices, the future of the towers might have been completely different, which strikingly reveals the influence public institutions can have in durably shaping the building standards on the level of a city or a whole region.

74   Following the coffered ceiling test, the next step was to find an elegant window solution to bring natural ventilation into the new building while respecting the 1.5 m grid of the existing façade, which was appreciated for its proportion and openness. A sliding window, opening up to a maximum of 11 cm, made it possible to maintain these qualities without the need for a balustrade. Ultimately, negotiations with contractors regarding price and performance led to another solution for the final design.

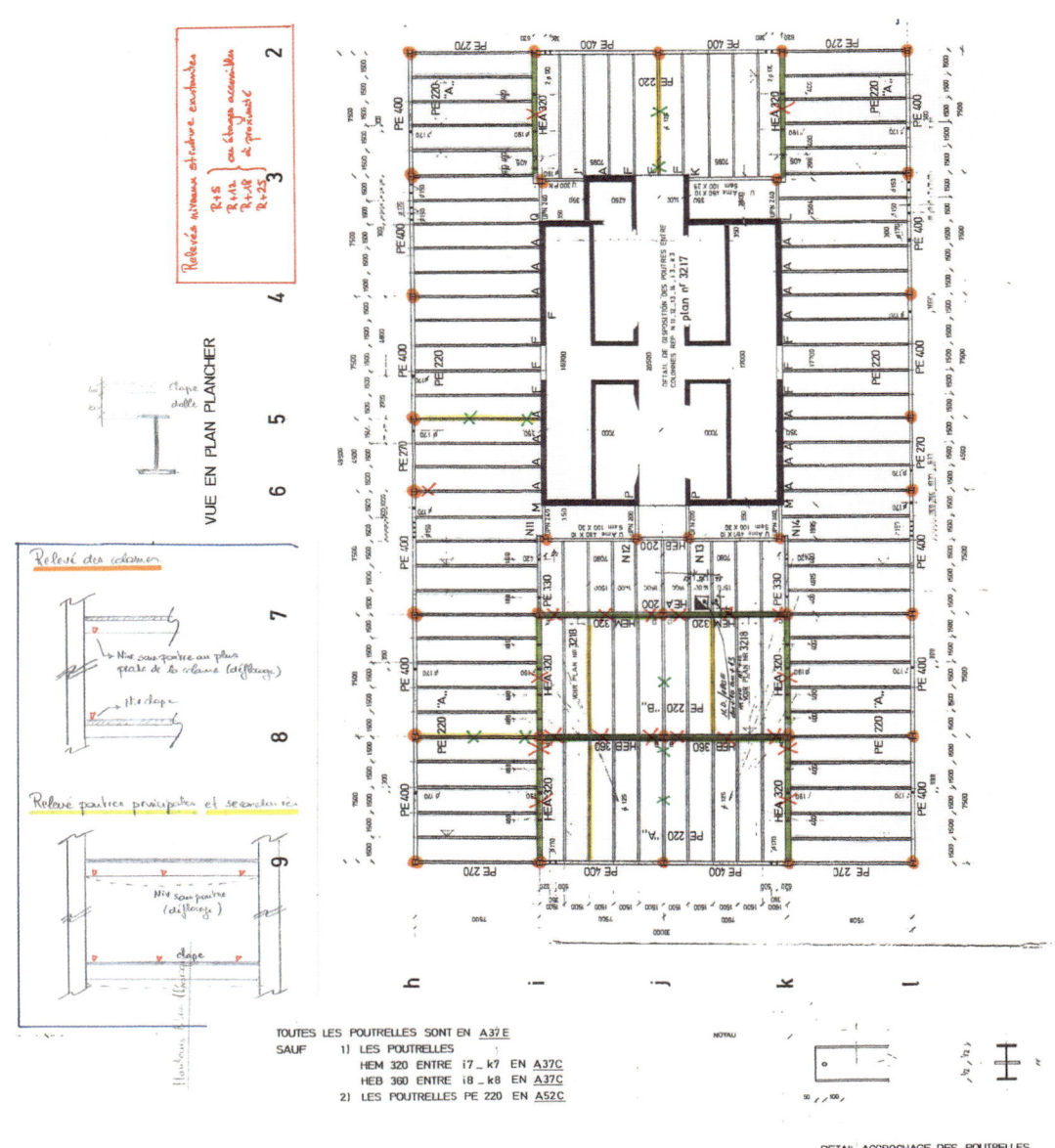

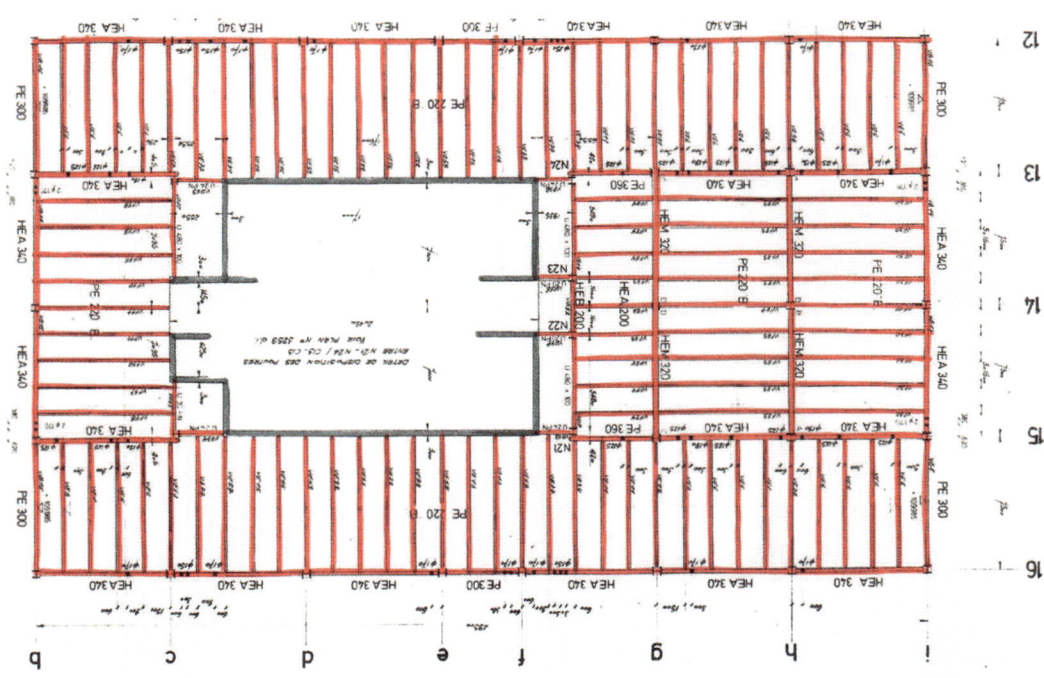

75　　Structural plan of a typical floor of the existing towers, with annotations by the structural engineer surveying the major deformations of the light steel and concrete floor slabs around the concrete cores.

THE CITY AS A MINE

With the awareness of the massive contribution of the construction sector to the ongoing global environmental crisis, the revision of our modes of access to building materials has become unavoidable. Disused buildings should therefore no longer be regarded as containing waste, but rather as containing valuable building materials, making the city a de facto mine harboring a wealth of elements to be reincorporated into new structures.

The former WTC was approached with this mindset and was dismantled consciously. Before the partial demolition started, Brussels-based architects and 'un-builders' Rotor stripped the building of its valuable fittings and materials (stone slabs, door handles, light fixtures, signage, etc.) to be made available to buyers for other building projects. Other less valuable components such as insulation sheets or floorings were also removed and sold.

In the course of the project, however, it became apparent that reusing the building's own materials for the transformed building might not be the best solution, as it would involve storing large volumes for several years between demolition and rebuilding.

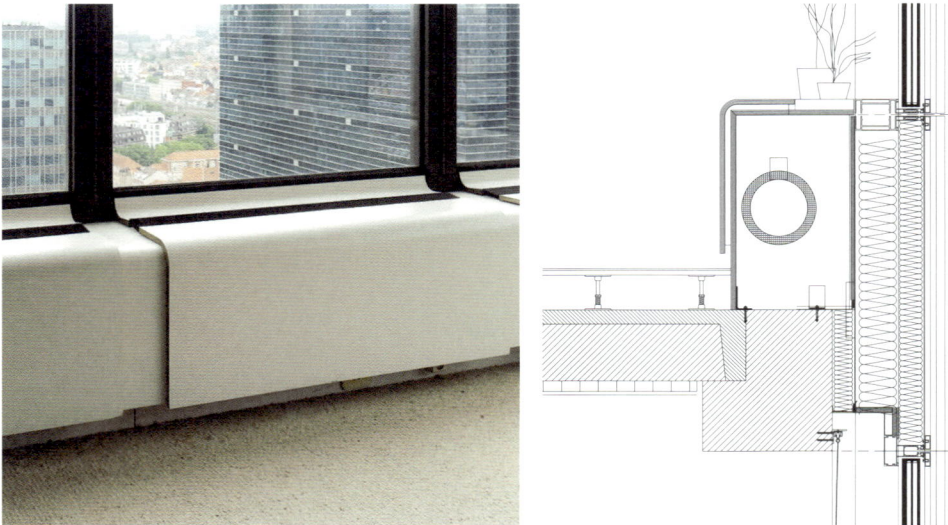

76–77 In April 2019 the radiator covers were removed. As a similar element was needed for the new project, an attempt to reuse them was proposed. Tests were carried out to evaluate the feasibility, as they needed to be cleaned, sanded down, and trimmed. This ultimately made their reuse more expensive than buying new ones, and the solution was scrapped. Yet it functioned as a significant learning process about how to efficiently integrate reclaimed elements in future designs. Dismantled by Rotor, these covers were later reused for several furniture projects.

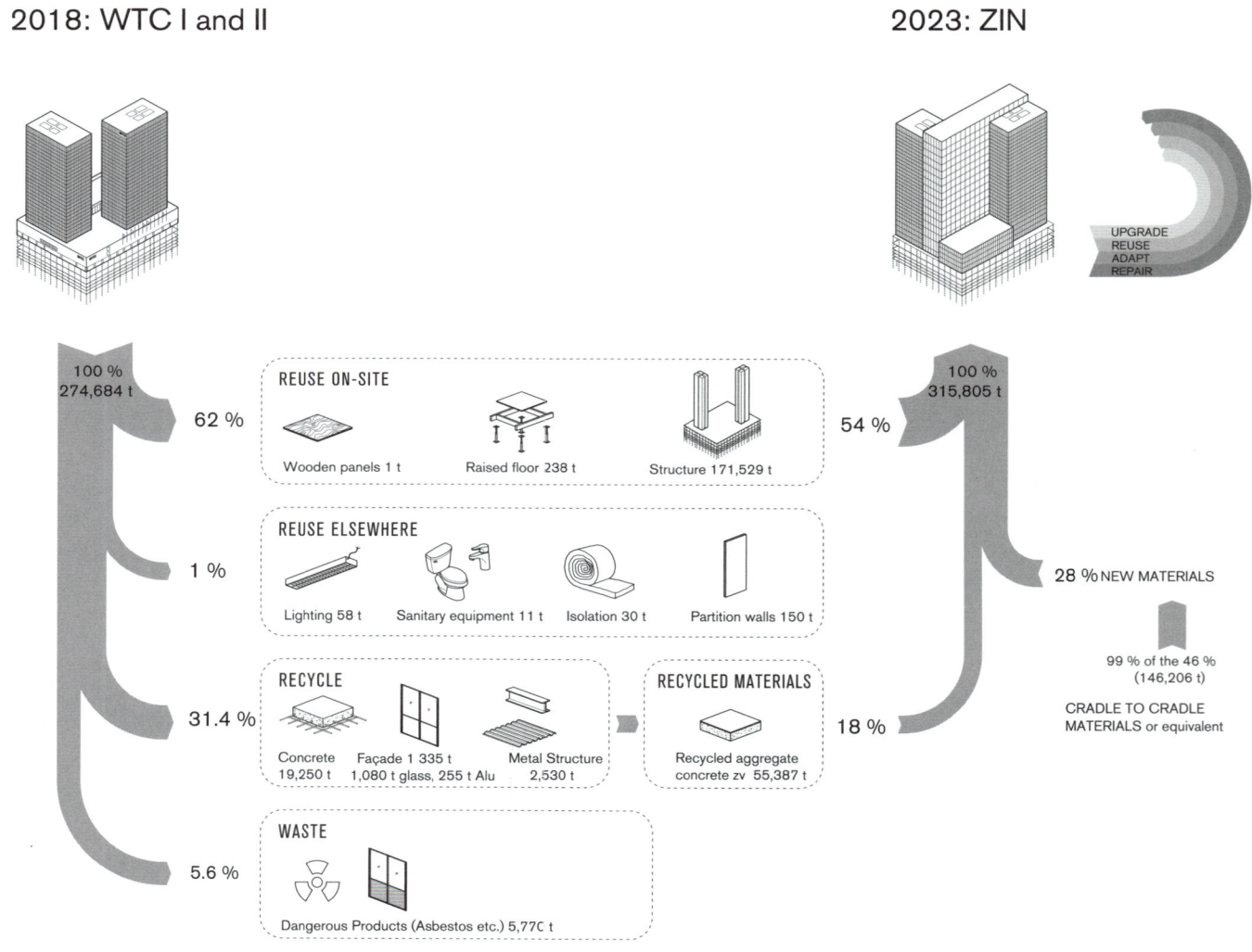

2018: WTC I and II

2023: ZIN

UPGRADE
REUSE
ADAPT
REPAIR

100 %
274,684 t

100 %
315,805 t

62 %   54 %

REUSE ON-SITE
Wooden panels 1 t   Raised floor 238 t   Structure 171,529 t

1 %

REUSE ELSEWHERE
Lighting 58 t   Sanitary equipment 11 t   Isolation 30 t   Partition walls 150 t

28 % NEW MATERIALS

99 % of the 46 %
(146,206 t)

CRADLE TO CRADLE
MATERIALS or equivalent

31.4 %

RECYCLE
Concrete 19,250 t   Façade 1 335 t 1,080 t glass, 255 t Alu   Metal Structure 2,530 t

RECYCLED MATERIALS
Recycled aggregate concrete zv 55,387 t

18 %

5.6 %

WASTE
Dangerous Products (Asbestos etc.) 5,770 t

78 Scheme produced in December 2018 showing the material flows coming out of the existing building. A majority was maintained in the new project. Another portion was recycled (with some companies taking their products back to recycle them into new products of the same kind), while a small portion of toxic materials had to be disposed of and processed.

79–80 The rubble of the concrete floor slabs of WTC I and II was collected during the demolition and brought to a recycling plant nearby Brussels by lorry. Here they were ground down, graded, and cleaned, giving 3,500 tons of ABR high-value A+ aggregate. These aggregates were then transported to the concrete plant and used for the new floor compression layers, floor plates, and prefabricated elements.

81 All materials without reuse purpose were separated from their composition with other materials during the demolition process and afterward recycled to raw materials

82 The numerous slabs of Carrara marble that covered the public reception space of the bank located inside WTC I and II are now available to buy through Rotor's reclaimed building products store.

83 The WTC's gypsum boards were salvaged and reused in a nearby Steiner school.

84 The entire roof of the towers' plinth was covered in typical Silex tiles, used as an economical terrace cladding until today. After being cleaned with a high-pressure water jet, these 50-year-old tiles are as good as new and will be reused for the loggias for both offices and apartments of ZIN.

MATERIALENPASPOORT - NIEUWE SITUATIE

85 This material passport was developed by the Flemish Government and used for the first time in their public tender for their new offices. It is close to a traditional bill of quantity but focuses on the circular qualities and health properties of each material used in the project. It results in a grade given to the project out of 100 points and calculated based on weight rather than on square meters or item count. The origin of elements, their certification, and their capacity for disassembly are also important criteria.

EXPANDED RESPONSIBILITY

Circular thinking not only relies on an intelligence to be deployed at the time of construction, but also on an anticipation of the future life of the building, leading to a simultaneous reflection on construction and space, and on a new and overarching material responsibility.

All the elements used in the fit-out of the new towers will therefore be assembled in a reversible way, making it easy to carry out adaptation works or to take them apart and reuse them should the building's life cycle reach an end. In addition, all building components, old and new, are fully mapped and consigned into a 'material passport' available to both owner and tenant—a document listing all products and elements used in the project, as well as their specifications, dimensions, instructions for installation, repair, or dismantling and reuse. A way for the building to retain its knowledge through time, independently from the design team, and to hopefully convert this knowledge into durability.

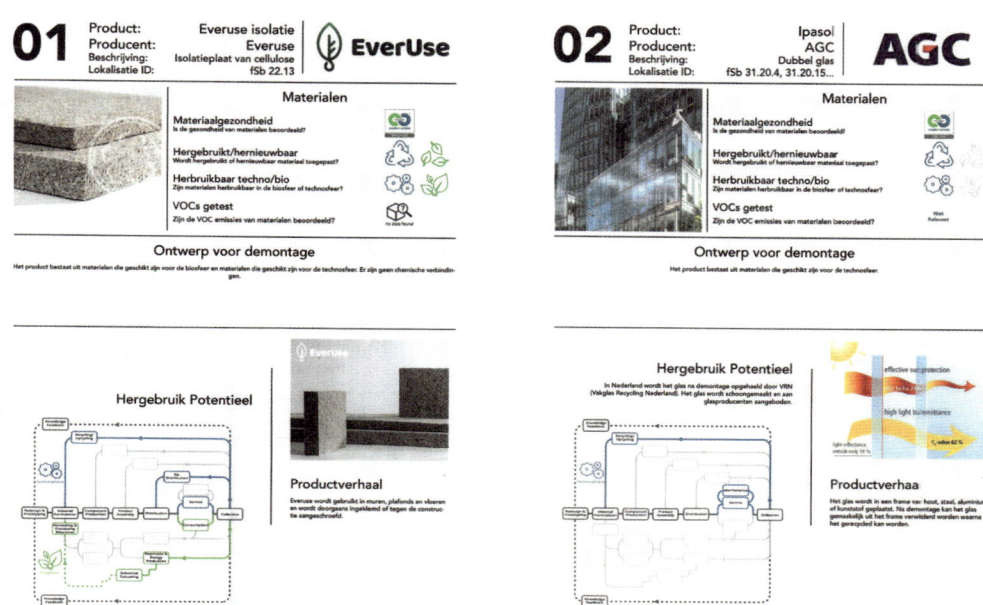

86–87 Product sheets, as conceived by Drees & Sommer and EPEA, showing how the abstract materials and elements entered in the material passport exist on the market.

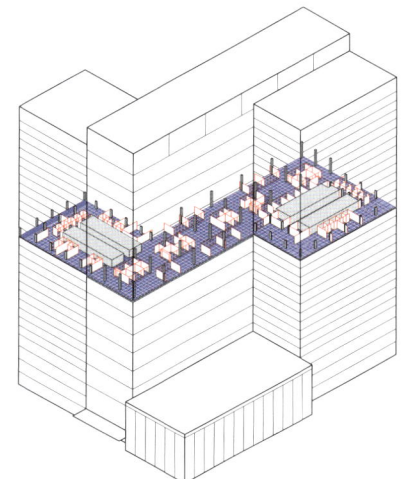

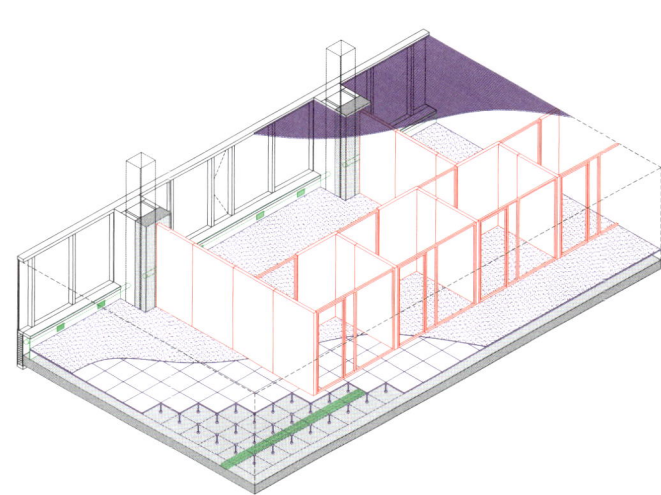

88 The building's 7.5 × 7.5 m structural grid is further subdivided into a 75 × 75 cm grid for the interior design elements of the offices, also coinciding with the façade's 1.5 × 1.5 m module. These measurements are a factor of one another, which makes them interchangeable in the building.

89 Within the building's lasting, concrete framework, shorter-lived fittings are installed, as well as light partitions that can easily be installed or dismantled to adapt to variations in needs.

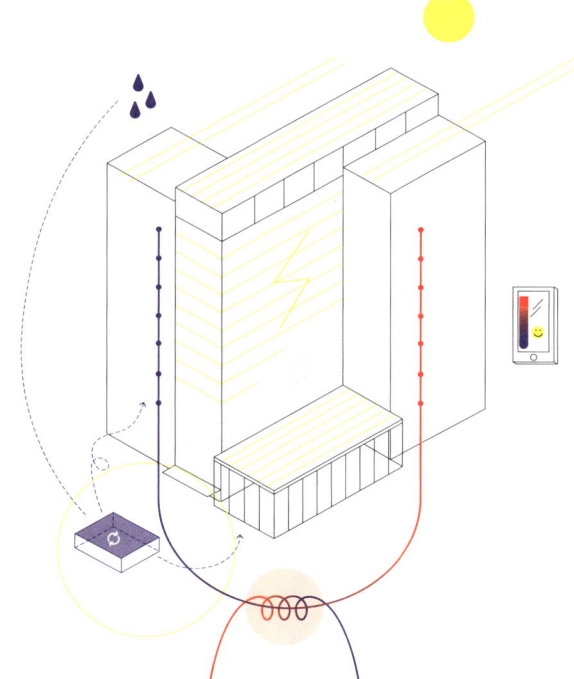

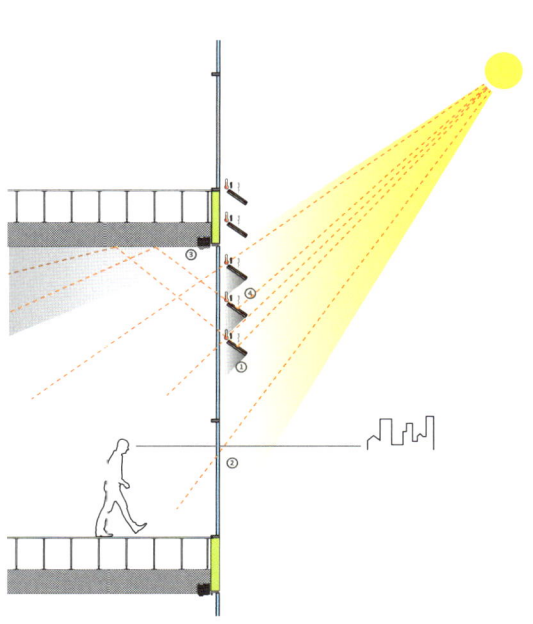

90 Like the flows of materials, energy and water are exchanged between the building and its environment. Energy is recuperated before being shared again between different programs, all tapping into the same loop to ensure minimal loss of the energy consumed by the building.

91 Energy production scheme based on photovoltaic louvers also serving as sun shading for the double-height floors.

A VERSATILE CONSTRUCTION

The more flexible and versatile a space, the more chances it has of being able to accommodate new types of occupations without needing drastic adaptations. Besides the constructive aspect, the spatial concept of the building was therefore also designed to maximize the duration of its life cycle.

A spatial idea of circularity illustrated by the Volume Capable, which, by offering double-height spaces and expanding the maximum surface of each plateau, introduces a new scale in the neighborhood and offers increased versatility and transformability to the building. In a similar direction, the side of the tower facing the nearby park was given loggias without differentiating housing and office levels. This decision was much debated with the commissioners but allowed for a potential future in which the offices could all be converted into housing while offering generous and unusual outside spaces to the offices in the meantime.

The floor slabs are all topped up by a technical floor, making it possible to integrate the insulation and the different kinds of networks and ducts needed by the different users of the building. Here again, those technical floors allow reversibility, or fluctuation, and therefore foster hybridity in time, as well as an overall resilience for the building as framework, making sure it is not at risk of being demolished in a near future because of its limitations.

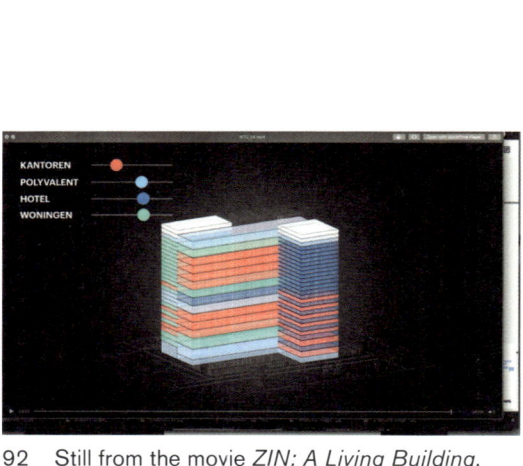

92 Still from the movie *ZIN: A Living Building*, showing how programs could evolve over time without the need to modify the architecture.

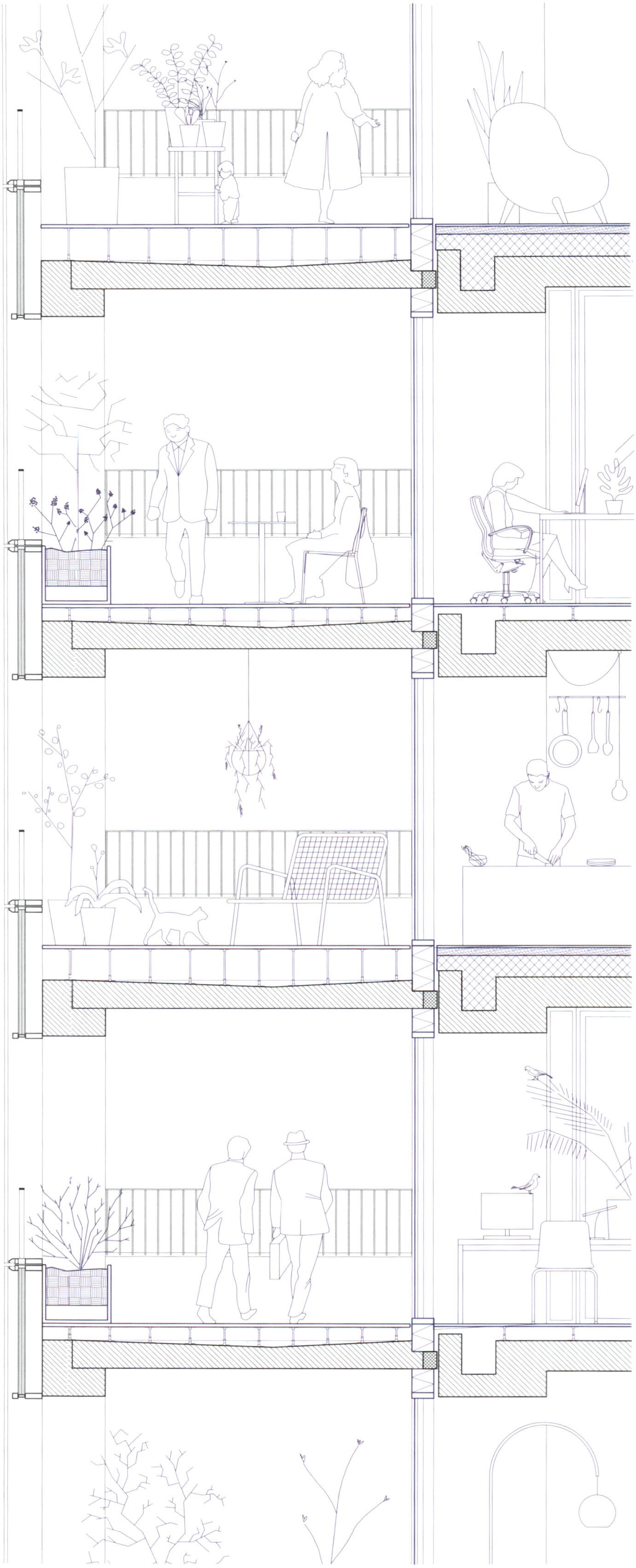

93 Detailed section of the large terraces toward the park, where employees and residents alike will be able to enjoy the view and evening sun.

5. CARE AND CURATE

ZIN will function as a prototype of what the Northern Quarter could become and the type of habitat that could be built there. An attempt at defining a new type of urbanity, one that is no longer about monolithic buildings standing in isolation but about hybrid urban objects activating their surroundings, functioning as extensions of the public space and having a beneficial urban, social, and ecological impact.

The project, treated as five volumes (the two towers, the Volume Capable, the greenhouse, and the co-working space), takes up its role as a de facto city block, with its lower buildings mediating between its towering proportions and the street. The lobby of the offices is moved to the first floor as a piano nobile, which allows many different functions and addresses to occupy the ground floor, creating a diverse ground floor that serves as an interface used both by users in the building and by users of the neighborhood.

The gradient from inside to outside, from private to collective to public, is accompanied by new scales and forms of vegetation, giving a new identity to the environment. This approach gives a new meaning to the large-scale spaces that are so characteristic to the district, creating a new continuity from the boulevard over the Volume Capable to the private terraces, in an attempt to qualify the 'emptiness' in a new way, connecting people and biodiversity.

With this ambition, and beyond this singular building, the idea of transformation of the neighborhood, of a 'Habitat North,' remains a long-term project, relying on offering new and improved spaces, on an enhanced relation to indoor and outdoor ecologies, but also a continued engagement and care.

94   During the temporary occupation, plants were installed in response to the different climatic conditions found on the generic floors, ranging from more arid on the southeast corner to more humid on the northwest.

KEY DATES	ACTORS	KEY STEPS
Spring 2018	Community North Collective	Urban roof garden
01/06/2018	Pool Is Cool	North beach
June 2018	51N4E / l'AUC / Jaspers-Eyers / Plant en Houtgoed	ZIN greenhouse development
June 2018	LabNorth, perspective. brussels, BMA	Conference 'North District, Next Step?'
07/09/2020	LabNorth	Mobile forest
November 2020	perspective. brussels	Public survey on 'A Shared Vision for Territory North'
November 2021	perspective. brussels	Diagnostic of 'A Shared Vision for Territory North'
January 2022	perspective. brussels	Second public survey and information session on 'A Shared Vision for Territory North'
19/04/2022	LabNorth	Demineralization project for the end of Boulevard du Roi Albert II

A PUBLIC ENVIRONMENT

The lower levels of ZIN have been designed as an open and public building, an urban system based on a continuity between the city and a ground floor conceived as a varied interior world. The socle manifests the building's various identities while establishing a strong connection with the surrounding streets and park which the World Trade Center used to turn its back to. This was achieved by placing the entrance level of the offices (the main occupant of the building) on the first floor of the building, leaving space on the ground floor for multiple and varied occupations. The project thus multiplies access points to the different programs, distributing them all around the building's perimeter.

Inside this public environment, combinations of greenery and bespoke pieces of furniture were designed as a necessary complement to the little-defined framework of the building and as a way to mediate relations between the building and its users. Those free-standing assemblages construct the next level of the project and strengthen the building's public character. The minimal shell is thus given a further specification, creating an inviting atmosphere for the current use while retaining the mutability of the building.

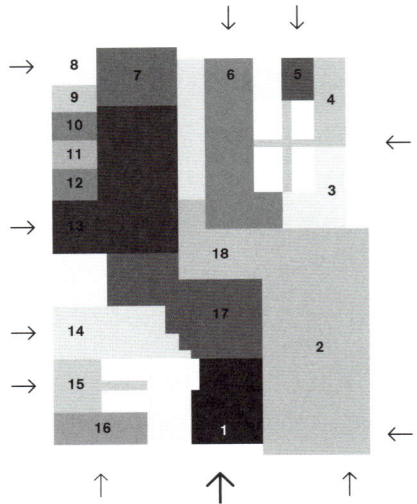

95   Scheme showing the building as an urban block, with a multitude of individual addresses directly connecting to the surrounding streets. A clear intention to move away from the 'single address logic' based on a large entrance lobby or atrium from which the whole distribution of the building is then organized.

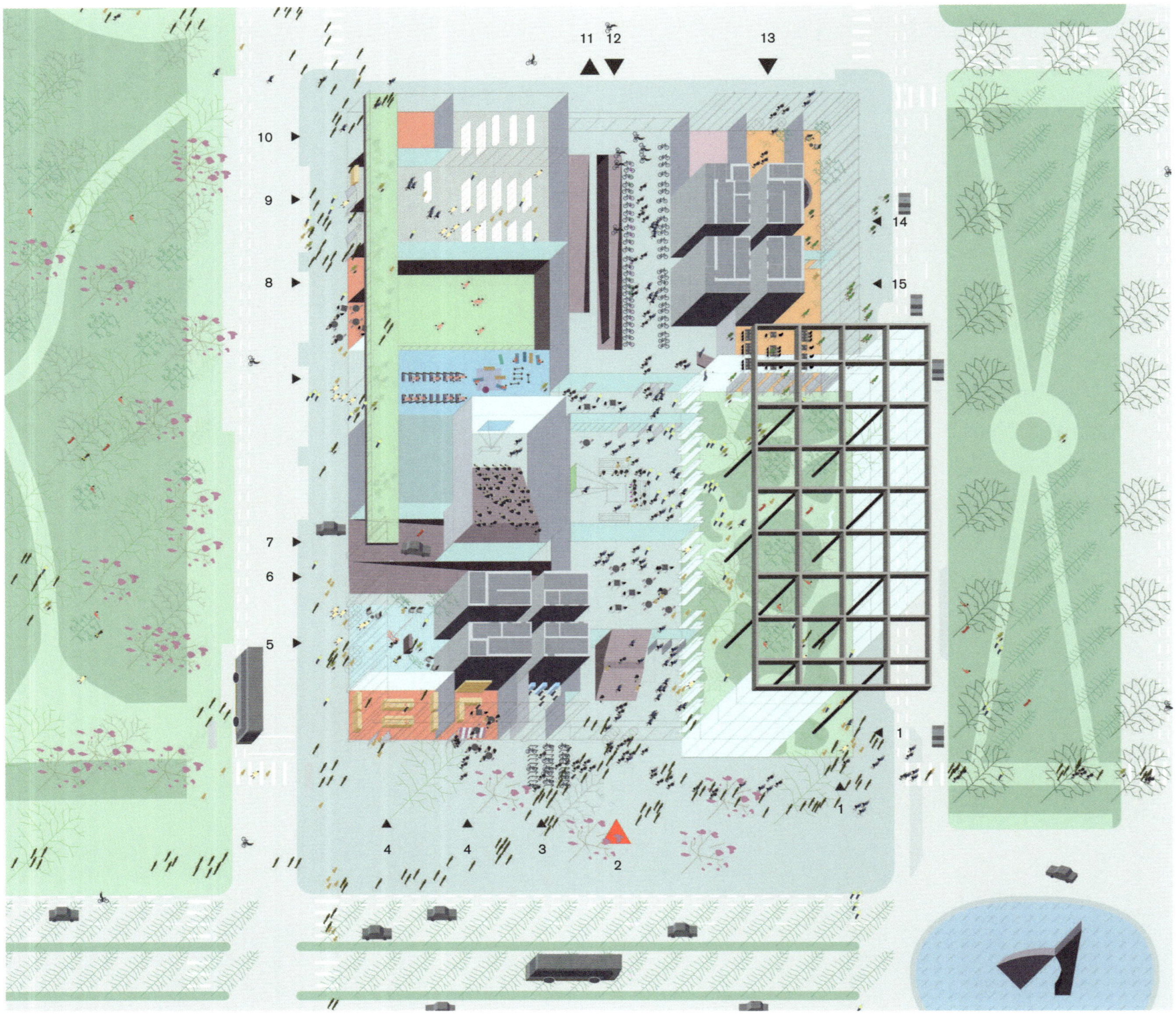

96   Axonometric drawing of the ground floor showing the variety of programs accommodated by this level: (1) greenhouse, (2) entrance hall leading to the offices, (3) access to public parking garage, (4) shops, (5) entrance hall leading to the apartments, (6) loading and unloading zone, (7) access to parking garage, (8) access to sports and event hall, (9) access to supermarket, (10) access to activities center, (11) exit from parking garage, (12) bicycle storage, (13) entrance courtyard, (14) hotel lobby, (15) hotel bar and restaurant.

97–99 Arriving from the large staircase, the first part of the entrance level of the Flemish Government's offices is focused on the reception of both public and employees (top image). A large greenery installation, like a forest of loose pots, acts as a divider. It elaborates on a test setup which was installed in 51N4E's offices, both to show the impact such a vegetal assemblage could have and to test the combination of species (middle image). Behind this green installation, the back of the entrance level accommodates a co-working and lunch area where strips of greenery further divide the space for increased intimacy (bottom image).

BUILDING AS ECOSYSTEM

The temporary occupation was used by landscape architects Plant en Houtgoed to test the influence that plants could have on a typical office ecosystem, air quality, and atmosphere. This integrated treatment of greenery was picked up in the design as an element creating an identity for the building's collective spaces. A kind of 'green thread' modulated into a series of interventions: a public greenhouse on the ground floor as a buffer space between city and tower; a green scheme for the office floors; a 'green façade' created by the loggias overlooking the park; and finally a huge roof garden on top of the central volume.

The early modernist dream of living in towers standing in vegetation is evoked in the project but has been turned inside out, with the greenery being brought indoors. The vegetation in the central volume acts as an image of the public domain continuing inside the entrance level of the offices on the first floor and then throughout the whole volume. Each double-height floor is equipped with built-in pits, making it possible to grow up to twenty trees, the technical floor becoming the facilitator of a vegetal life. The pits will be supplemented with loose potted plants that can be arranged and rearranged to create filters and be moved around according to the seasons, changing the spatial impression of the offices accordingly.

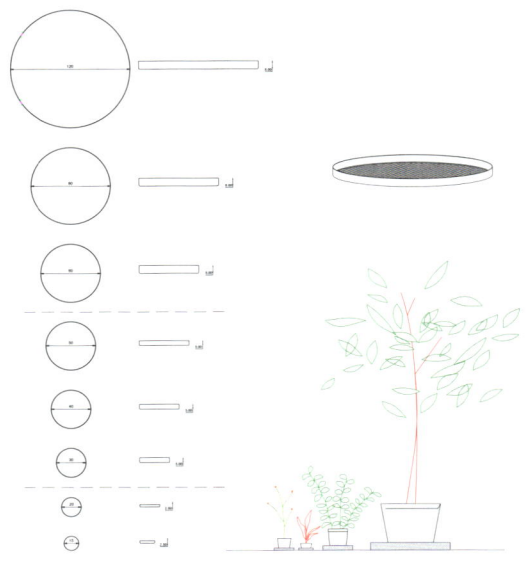

100   Simple trays of varying sizes were developed as a base on which to set all potted plants in the building.

101   There are four types of ecosystems in the building, each characterized by its own species and experience: (1) public greenhouse, (2) green park façade, (3) interior forest, (4) panoramic roof garden.

102

103–104 During the temporary occupation of WTC I, Plant en Houtgoed created interior plant installations to experiment on the way different species behaved in an office climate. Among other tests: a humid room inhabited by birds and a cactus composition in a drier meeting room.

NEW URBAN RELATIONS

While the main entrance of the WTC was situated on Boulevard du Roi Albert II, the 'historical' and monumental road of the Manhattan Plan, the main entrance of ZIN, leading to the offices, was purposely located on Boulevard Simon Bolivar, a road going from the Brussels-North station straight to the Tour & Taxis urban redevelopment site on the other side of the canal. This anchors the building in this newly enhanced urban thoroughfare cutting through rail, road, and canal, and further strengthens the east-west connection needed in the center of Brussels.

This transversal direction also connects to new architectural and urban hubs such as the soon-to-be-opened Kanal-Centre Pompidou as well as to greenery and water, like the Maximilian Park and the Tour & Taxis Park across the canal and the Senne River, which is soon to be uncovered.

This relation to an immediate urban environment turns the building into a place of overlaps between local life and metropolitan scale, in which users coming from the area, the rest of the city, or commuting from the Flemish Region cross each other's paths.

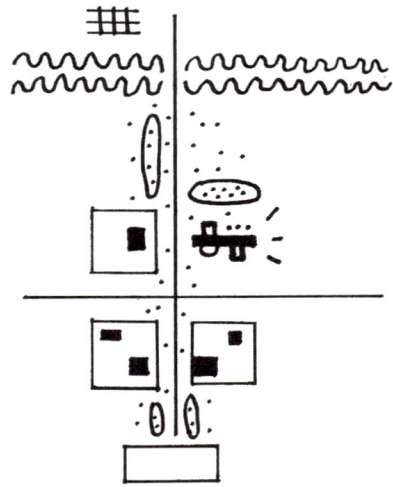

105 The project's urban intention: forgoing the monolithic plinth and creating a building that relates to and interacts with its surroundings in differentiated ways.

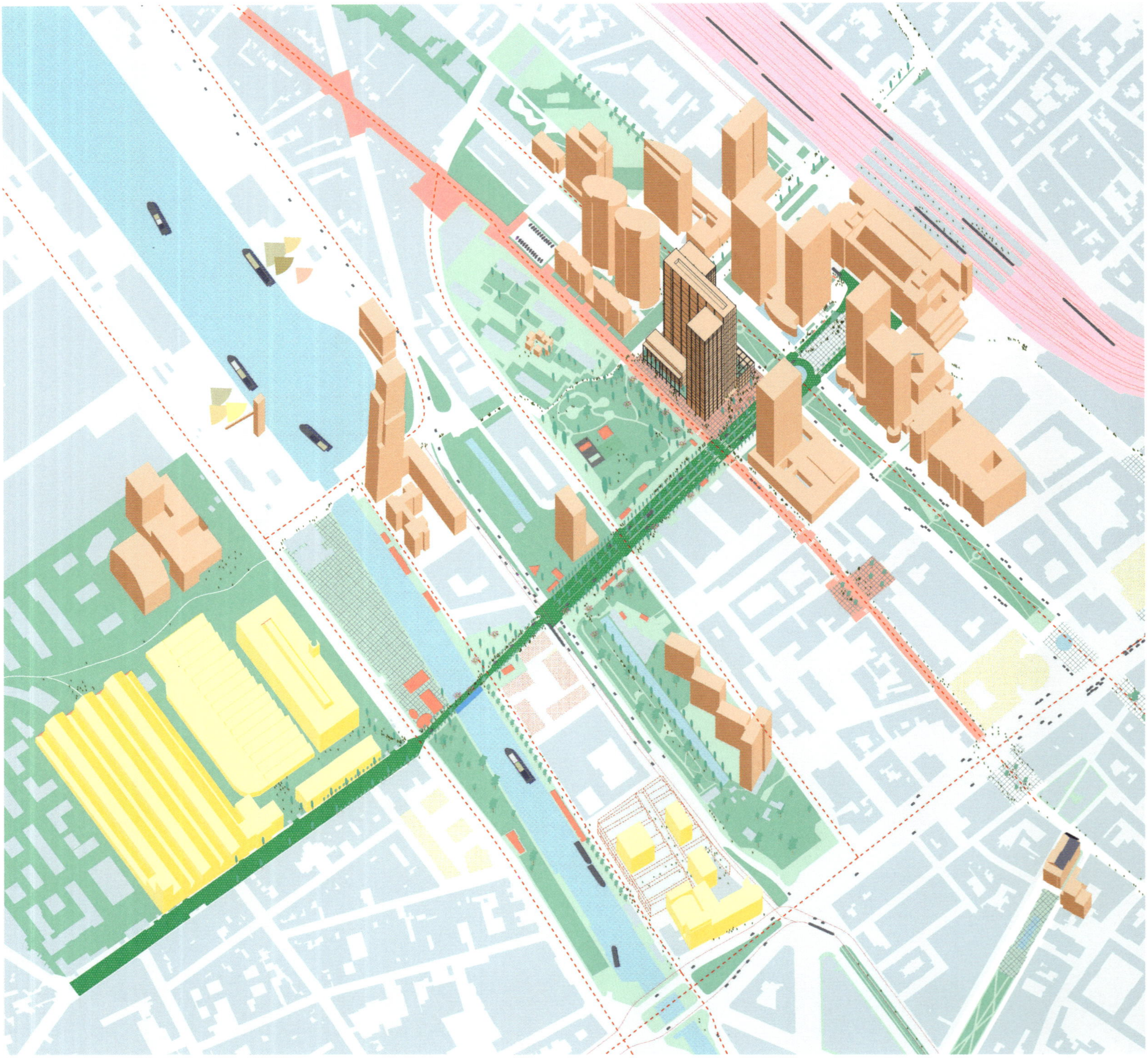

106 'Urban Reality Drawing' by 51N4E to represent the project and its embedding in its surroundings.

107   On top of the building, a covered garden spans the whole surface of the new Volume Capable and is activated by a restaurant belonging to the hotel. As such, it will offer the first public rooftop destination within the Northern Quarter.

108   On the west side of the project, a mainly residential street runs along the building. While the hermetic plinth of WTC I and II acted as an abrupt interruption in the row of residential façades, the new lower volume now addressing that side responds to the housing blocks by mimicking their mid-rise scale and light concrete hues.

109–110   The ground floor's polyvalent spaces are designed to be accessible not only from the offices themselves but also from the street or greenhouse. This will make it possible for them to be used more flexibly, at different times and by different users.

A LONG-TERM PROCESS

Habitat North is a long-term promise to the neighborhood, one that is not just about architecture but also about people's long-standing involvement.

This change of mindset is reflected, for instance, in LabNorth's continued engagement to prolong temporary occupations and the testing of architectural, urban, or landscape solutions. But also in the consideration by the Flemish Government to commission Congolese artist Jean Katambayi Mukendi, not for a single monumental artwork, but for an eighteen-year-long residency during which he would interact with the building and neighborhood.

The hotel situated in ZIN will be operated by the Standard, whose CEO has lived and worked in Brussels in the past, and who sees potential for development of the Northern Quarter, as he did when he was first to settle on the New York High Line or when he opened a hotel in the heart of the Los Angeles business district. An implantation that could create leverage to improve the area's future, along with the many initiatives happening in parallel on all levels.

112   Projected atmosphere of the hotel's ground-floor lobby.

113   View of the publicly accessible and shared roof garden.

111   Visit of the existing towers with the CEO of the Standard.

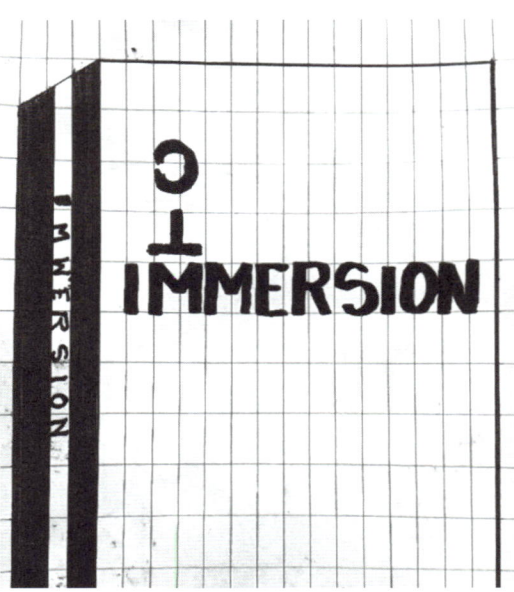

114–115   The process of integrating art in the building has been pushing the boundaries of how such an intervention can take shape. The proposal made by the curators Valerie Verhack and Hilde Teerlinck was to invite an artist to occupy and produce work in the building over the same period of time as the lease the Flemish Government has, namely eighteen years. They imagined that over this period of time, the artist would engage with the place and its residents, indeed almost becoming one of the residents, alongside the civil servants. In this proposal, the artist would grow along with the building becoming the venue where not only the art but also the evolution of an artistic career becomes present. Despite general enthusiasm about this idea, its practical application bumped into too many legal and procedural constraints, and the shift from 'art as product' toward 'art as presence' unfortunately didn't survive, even if it did produce a very sharp and engaged discussion on the role of artistic interventions beyond mere decoration, revealing important questions about how a building can live and be lived in. In the screenshot of the online meeting, the artist Jean Katambayi Mukendi shows his own workshop, openly reflecting about what it would mean to have a 'dependance' in the former World Trade Center in Brussels.

HOW TO PRODUCE CHANGE?

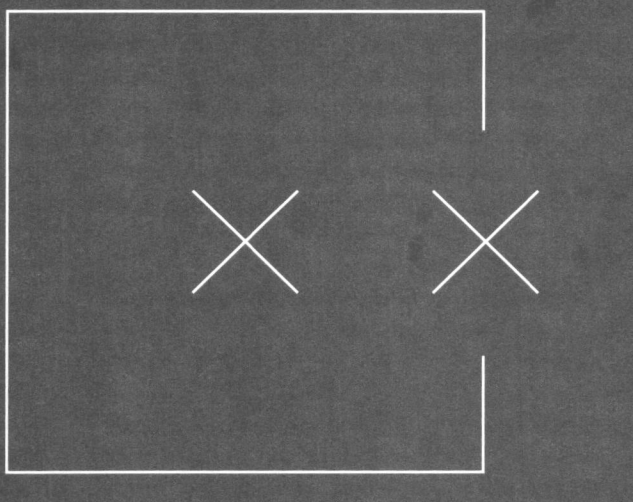

Reflection from Inside Reflection from In Between Reflection from Outside

A CADAVRE EXQUIS FOR A NEW PROCESS OF TRANSFORMATION

Conversation in the Same Bubble

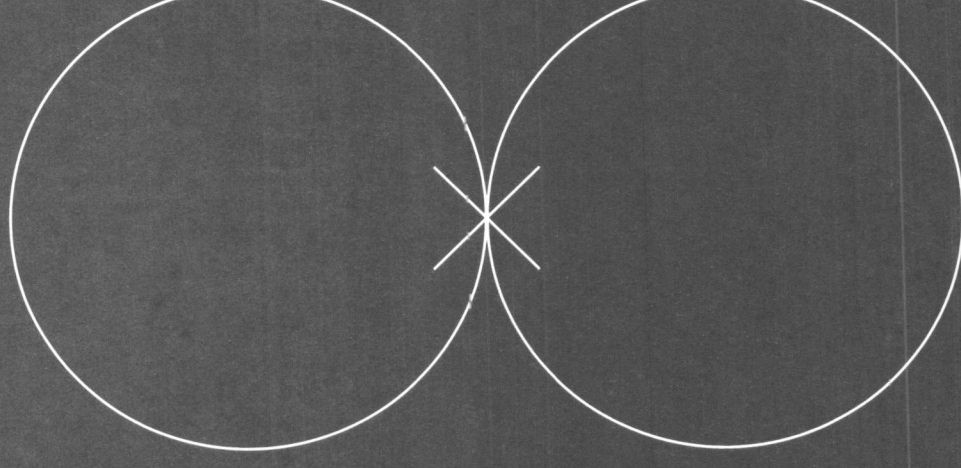

Conversation between Different Bubbles

Urban Lake proposed for the Northern Quarter, totaling 200,000 m³ of water. Student project by Johan Anrys, Bart Hollanders, Natalie Vanderick, and Petrus Walraet, published in *Archis*, April 1996.

EDITORIAL NOTE

Let us start by saying this. The transformation of the World Trade Center (WTC) did not create a method or 'best practice' that can easily be explained, repeated, or labeled. It was messy in multiple ways. The process got contested on different fronts, from within and outside. Some consider it the greatest achievement in architectural and urban renewal in Brussels in years, others the biggest sellout to conservative real estate. The following texts offer insight into the different opinions expressed and inquiries made during the period of 2017 until 2021 in the context of the WTC and, to a larger extent, Brussels. We conversed and interviewed stakeholders at the very start of the process, during the temporary use of the WTC, and later, when the transformation to ZIN was happening. We drew lessons from this process and formulated five learning points in the center spread of this booklet. By no means does this compilation provide a complete overview, nor is it without bias. It reflects, from different angles and in different time frames, on the questions at stake, and foremost invites others to continue the conversation and join the discussion.

Freek Persyn

From WTC to ZIN: The Uncoordinated Constellation That Produced Change

After so many years of silent neglect, how did it happen that the World Trade Center (WTC) in Brussels was ready to be revamped with so much energy and passion? Even if it still seems too early to celebrate, the contrast is striking between the decades of disinterest and silent status quo that the Northern Quarter came to stand for and the sudden energy and ambition the refurbishment of the WTC now radiates. As if a bottle of champagne had been fermenting for many years and had now suddenly burst open and was bubbling all over the place.

The first champagne moment of the WTC, half a century ago, did not spark what was dreamed of. We hope—and feel the responsibility—to try more and better now. It is great to be re-energized, and it is equally important to keep asking ourselves why a place that seemed prone to mediocrity can suddenly be ambitious on multiple levels, a game changer pushing the boundaries of what was thought possible. Is it perhaps the emblematic character of the WTC that spoke to the imagination and drove everyone to go beyond their own expectations? That is undoubtedly true, but it is not the whole answer.

What has happened with the WTC project is a fortunate alignment of conditions that created a window of opportunity to shoot for excellence. This alignment was a matter of chance, and luckily there were enough people that were alert enough to see the opportunity and push for it to become fact. It is the story of a smart investor, an invested client, a massive community of temporary users, an unlikely alliance between dedicated architects and engineers, and an engaged group of policymakers, all working together in a constellation that was to a large extent dependent on chance.

The aim of this text is not to turn the project into a best practice—there is too much contingency for that—but to try and unpack the conditions that produced the change—and to describe what

partial dynamics were at play, and potentially see the prototype of the process this constellation of lucky stars is making, and to ask whether it would be possible to favor the conditions for interesting constellations—of other stars, so to speak—that can challenge the status quo, including on sites and with buildings that are less emblematic than the WTC.

To understand this, multiple things have to be acknowledged that were happening at once, or rather that there were *enough* things happening so that a constellation could take shape. The refurbishment of the WTC came at a moment when different strategies were being tried out: 1) the on-site testing of a hybrid work environment that created a temporary common ground for confronting others and learning from them; 2) an ambitious tender for office spaces of the Flemish Government and its sustainable development framework (GRO); and 3) the *chambre de qualité* of the Brussels Government Architect (BMA) and Urban.Brussels in preparation of the building permit to transform the towers. Even if these different dynamics were coming from different angles, in the case of the transformation of the WTC they coincided in time and place and started to connect and amplify each other. In all their messiness and without being coordinated, they created favorable conditions for a radical change.

The first and most charming dynamic was the temporary occupation, which drew together a large group of actors from many different backgrounds. The temporary use was an experiment, a 1:1 mock-up of a piece of Hybrid Business District or, to put it more bluntly, a demonstration that the generic floors of the WTC did not have to be used in a generic way. This experiment was set up as a real-life test of an idea proposed already in 2011 in the study of Brussels 2040, itself inspired by the Shibuya University program in Tokyo. Back then, the generic spaces of the Northern Quarter were imagined as the ideal platform for metropolitan diversity. The question of the mock-up was: why couldn't the large-scale structures of the WTC towers be seen as an infrastructure for a fine-grained diversity of users and uses? This test was not about testing different programs, but rather about the diversity that could be found within what is normally understood as one type of program: the workspace.

With the temporary use, in a short time span different forms of professional use collided, the sociocultural, educational, and creative sectors rubbed up against each other, and a whole range of public and collective events took place. The fact that space was provided in exchange for the running costs and in return for actions in and on the Northern Quarter spurred a wildly diverse series of interventions. It ranged from a clumsy but inviting sandpit made with beer crates to an impressive *pool performance* in the roundabout's water feature by Pool Is Cool and Alive Architecture. None of this was really coordinated or steered. Sometimes it was even hardly enabled. The different people involved in the process (including ourselves) did not always understand what was really happening, nor what it all meant. At most, it was

Is it possible to consider this circumstantial *cadavre exquis* as a critical condition for success? We might all agree that it cannot be a formula that can be repeated. Nevertheless, it challenges urban planning and its unhealthy focus on order. What this situation reveals is that in situations of stasis, the focus on creating disorder (the temporary occupation) can be as helpful as the focus on order.

a chaotic and lively environment, a swarming and informal set of encounters and micro-discussions and confrontations. Since this common environment was not curated, many different things were being tried out and questioned at once. There were opinions and counter-opinions, different ideas and desires formulated, and things were tested for real, on the spot. Although haphazard, it became a fertile ground for a critical and polyphonic dialogue.

It was striking to see how this on-site mock-up was also piercing holes in the bubble that real-estate circles are often accused of being. The team of Befimmo—already working for years to change their corporate culture from the inside out—was opening up to other opinions and viewpoints. And beyond the discourse and ideas, there was the enthusiasm. It was exhilarating to be part of this messy vitality and to be lifted up by its energy. It is not a coincidence that the project's new name became 'ZIN in Noord' (Dutch for 'Longing for North'), a name which reflects this energy.

A second dynamic—which was for the actual architectural transformation of the WTC, therefore clearly the most important dynamic—was the tender and the importance it gave to the sustainable development framework (GRO) of the Flemish Government. Named after the former Norwegian prime minister Gro Brundtland, this framework is a very extensive checklist of possible choices one can make to achieve a sustainable project. Choices one *can* make, not *should* make. The framework is indeed a measuring device and evaluation framework, more focused on encouraging than on imposing. It does so by showing aspects that can be acted upon. It focuses on an accumulation of multiple sustainable actions, some big, others small, putting the responsibility of choosing and integrating all of these possibilities in the hands of the design and build team. In some way,

the polyphony present in the temporary occupation found its twin in the design discussions. In the project atelier on the 15th floor of the WTC, there was a buzz of life on par with the energy that could be found on the other floors of the tower. Weighing up choices, positions, and possible impact, it all happened in a strict rhythm of weekly workshops, sometimes with up to 90 people present in parallel sessions, together producing integrated value. Here, the ample size of the floor and the informal availability of the space pushed people to liberate themselves and their work. There was no clean desk policy: the material remained on display, as a permanent collective brain at work, available for the whole team to see.

A third dynamic was the process established by the Brussels Government Architect and Urban. Brussels called the *chambre de qualité*. In line with its noble name, it took the shape of more formal rounds of presentation of the WTC tender proposal and its work-in-progress, which made it possible to verify the evolving relation between solutions and ambitions, negotiating both step by step. This consultation process was set up as an open dialogue on the design steps taken, sometimes with charged discussions on what was considered an improvement or not. At the start of this negotiation process was a candidacy procedure during which our team (51N4E and l'AUC) was selected on the basis of a set of overarching ambitions and an initial design proposal, i.e. the 'Volume Capable' connecting the towers. During the consultation process, both the ambitions and the design evolved. The ambitions expanded and became more refined, while the design itself got elaborated and was gradually verified. The topic of the ground floor became a real focus for the discussion, slowly but surely strengthening the way this big building might become a catalyst for the surrounding environment. Beyond the usual discussions about façade materials and urban silhouette—which generally dominate these types of commissions—there arose an affinity for the more structural and systemic aspects of the architecture: How many addresses would be created? How accessible would the ground floor really be? What would relations with the neighborhood be on all four sides? For the design team it required quite some stamina to show work that was not always entirely digested internally; for the *chambre de qualité* it was a difficult balance to strike between an attitude that now challenged, now supported, between engaging and keeping a distance. Over a series of sessions—on issues ranging from whether windows actually should open to how public the greenhouse should be—mutual trust grew. Step by step, leading up to the building permit, the gap between what was desirable and what was feasible was debated and gradually bridged. In the end, this dialogue process created a result that exceeded everyone's expectations.

Like a *cadavre exquis*, these three dynamics were never designed to work together, and yet their mutual presence and accidental interference made a difference. An activist learning environment confronting a Flemish framework for sustainable development, meeting a dialogue process run by the Brussels Government Architect and Urban.Brussels: this is the uncoordinated constellation that produced the change.[1]

The key question that arises is this: is it possible to consider this circumstantial *cadavre exquis* as a critical condition for success? We might all agree that it cannot be a formula that can be repeated. Nevertheless, it challenges urban planning and its unhealthy focus on order. What this situation reveals is that in situations of stasis, the focus on creating disorder (the temporary occupation) can be as helpful as the focus on order. It was as important to destabilize as it was to stabilize. In their simultaneity, the actions that have taken place created interactions that made it possible for new opportunities to arise. Without knowing what interactions to create or what opportunities will arise, it would help if urban planning would open up to that lack of control; to look in a more intimate way, not at a distant future, but to really engage with the now; not to place all hopes in a master plan but to create a framework that puts forward values that stimulate rather than regulate, to dare to dream and pursue goals beyond practicalities; and finally, not to claim to know the answers, but to dare to show vulnerability to enter into an open dialogue, and to question and reflect upon assumptions.

1. Challenging the inert situation in the Northern Quarter and going beyond the binaries that held it captive for so many years, the following diagram by Edgar Morin might be helpful, as it critically confronts the idea of progress and linearity that underlies the Northern Quarter when it was still called the Manhattan Plan. In this diagram—which Morin calls *tétralogique*—order, disorder, organization, and interactions are equally present. From a planning point of view, what the experience of going from WTC to ZIN shows us is that it might be good to start investing in all of them at once.

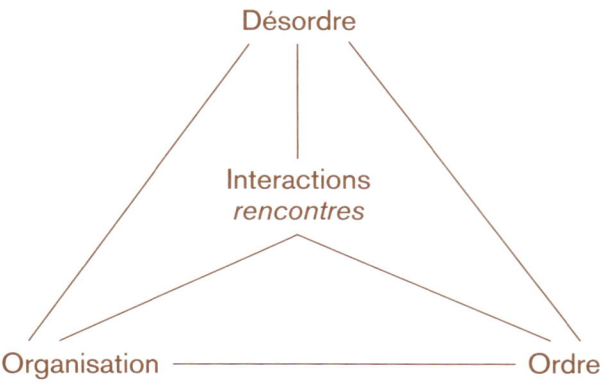

1. From: Edgar Morin, *La nature de la nature* (Paris: Seuil, 1977), 56.

Francesco Garutti, 'From within an Ecology of Practice,' *With and Within*, https://www.cca.qc.ca/en/articles/issues/28/with-and-within/73634/from-within-an-ecology-of-practice, last consulted: 22 April 2021.

'How do we return the fragments of Brussels's failed utopian World Trade Center to the city?'

Francesco Garutti

Djamel Klouche

Coincidences

WINTER NOTES ON SUMMER IMPRESSIONS, OR ZIN AS THE COINCIDENCE OF OPPOSITES

I like to use the term 'climates' to describe contemporary metropolitan phenomena. The notion of 'climate,' in the atmospheric sense of the term, could be a condition that articulates and mixes spatial issues, technical issues, societal issues, and above all cultural issues, in the image of the Crystal Palace, which in the nineteenth century provided a spatial and technical paradigm for the climatology of London, the emerging Great Industrial City. Already Dostoyevsky saw in it the pinnacle of the globalization of the Western world.

> The City with its millions and its universal trade, the Crystal Palace, the Universal Exhibition ... Yes, the Exhibition is staggering. You feel this terrifying force which has brought together here in a single herd all these infinite number of people from all over the world; you feel this titanic thought; you feel that something has been achieved here, that there is a victory, a triumph. ... It is all so solemn, so victorious, so proud that it becomes difficult to breathe. You look at these hundreds of thousands, these millions of people in the great streams flowing here, subdued, from all over the world—people who have all come with one thought, and who are crowding, noiselessly, stubbornly, and without saying anything, into this colossal palace, and you feel that it is there that something has definitely been accomplished, yes accomplished, completed.

> Fyodor Dostoyevsky, *Winter Notes on Summer Impressions*

At the same time, Walter Benjamin made Paris into the capital of the nineteenth century, with its Haussmannian passages and buildings over the city (another singular climatology combining technology, society, and culture). Another paradigm for the Wall Street city of New York was Manhattanism as described in the retroactive manifesto for Manhattan in Rem Koolhaas's book *Delirious New York*. The highways, shopping malls, and skyscrapers represented twentieth-century images of the concentration of a tertiary economy, as the iconic, generalized leisure spaces of a consumerist world that marked the later years of the last century, and as the spearhead of the dynamics of the sprawling city that we have inherited today.

We belong to a generation of architects who inherited this intertwined history, from which we have to invent new environments, new climatological arrangements. This was the fundamental question we faced when we embarked on this project in this modern part of Brussels.

It was truly remarkable to work on the transformation of WTC I and II, inside the building itself, even as its future was unfolding before our eyes. A light, simple, and immediate future, where communities mingled: student architects, architectural offices, dancers, graphic designers, to name but a few. Simultaneously, it was very easy to think about the building's future, as it was transforming before our eyes day after day as we immersed ourselves in it, but it was also extremely complicated since we were to some extent resisting the destruction of self-constructed energy, a form of the ecology of disorder, which drew improbable scenarios and anticipations.

I remain convinced that this dialectical or dialogical atmosphere—as Edgar Morin defines it—proved fertile for the ZEBRE hypothesis. The ZEBRE, an arrangement that probably unintentionally sought to rationalize the informal logistics generated by this building inhabited by hundreds of users who shared only one thing, the grandeur and fragility of a space. WTC I and II has become ZIN.

This ecology of disorder is also a 'coincidence of opposites,' an expression taken up by the passionate architect and teacher Oswald Mathias Ungers: it is what allows thought to go beyond itself, to progress from rational activity to an intellectual vision that opens up to renewed arrangements. The principle of non-contradiction prevents us from understanding and perceiving the plurality of worlds, yet today, the greatest challenge facing our profession as architects is to build and make plural climates coexist.

SOFT METROPOLITAN COLLECTOR

More than ten years ago, as we were reflecting on the Greater Paris project, we summoned the term *metropolitan collector*, which we defined at the time as the twenty-first-century Crystal Palace; the climatology of the contemporary city as a plural world.

> Outside central Paris, away from the airports or the Stade de France, there are very few large-scale, multiple buildings, open to all and non-exclusive, that structure the territory. There are only large shopping centres, great theme parks, and leisure areas to play this scouring role.

We wanted it to reflect what it aspired to be, a large territory open to a variety of uses that would contribute to the emergence of a new metropolitan ecology.

We need 21st century Crystal
Palaces, but what are they?
The Seine, the Stade de France,
the Louvre, Roissy, Les Halles,
the Château de Versailles.
They have the capacity to be the
drivers for mixed metropolitan
developments. They are discreet
but legible.
They are the void. They are the whole.
They are the place of movement.
They are sedimented spaces.
They are places of otherness, of
acceptance of the other, they
are non-exclusive.
They must foreshadow—just as
the Crystal Palace did in its time—
the urban mutations of contemporary society.
They penetrate into the pores and
holes of the metropolis to intensify
it from its most controversial sites.
They opt for hyper-accessibility
and diversity.
They are conscious of the societal
changes taking place before our
eyes and they immerse themselves
in those processes.
They are aware of the crises that
unfold before our eyes, and they
do not try to hide them. They anticipate the urban civilisation that is
emerging.
They are condensers of metropolitan
life. They are hetero-atmospheric.

AUC, *Grand Paris Stimulé, de la métropole
héritée aux situations parisiennes contempo-
raines*, 2009

We shared the same impertinence of wanting to build a prototype of a 'metropolitan collector,' a sort of world with a capital *W*, which was suffi-ciently powerful and stimulating to allow for the establishment of new interactions at its heart as well as fertile links and continuities with the sur-rounding evolving city.

We wanted it to reflect what it aspired to be, a large territory open to a variety of uses that would contribute to the emergence of a new metropoli-tan ecology.

To do this, we deliberately chose to exercise a high degree of freedom: the freedom to divide, to combine, to superimpose, to interpose, to under-line, to fill in, to complete, to order, to disorganize, and even to deconstruct. We sought all the tools to make a world that is gentle by virtue of its im-mediacy and directness; presumably, this perma-nent quest for a gentle contemporary urbanity as the future of the interwoven urban fabric of Brussels is what we sought here.

DESIGNING ZIN: AN URBANISM EXERCISE FOR METROPOLITAN USES

Designing ZIN was akin to the work of an urban planner in the noble sense of the term, one who challenges the very idea of the 'building' as a sin-gular and autonomous element in order to con-ceptualize the architectural project as a territory: a system with its own logistics that functions within the wider context of the metropolis, drawing ex-changes and alliances between the Gare du Nord, the canal spaces, and the dynamics of Tour et Taxis.

ZIN has become a receptacle of uses, from the large greenhouse that absorbs and unfurls the public space crossing from north to south, the circulation system that redistributes distinct func-tions and programs onto the existing cores, a large, capable, and generous volume that creates new ways of working, and the rooftop that turns into a balcony over the great Brussels landscape.

It was more like an urban planning exercise to put metropolitan uses and practices into perspec-tive than a classic architectural design process.

TRANSITION BY DESIGN: THE PROJECT OF TRANSFORMATION

If modern thought has indeed endeavored to order and arrange the world by species, function, and use, contemporary thought seeks to produce new arrangements in an ecological perspective. A philosophy of autonomous objects is replaced by a way of thinking that develops the plurality of worlds made up of interconnected objects. Everywhere, it becomes possible to inflect reality by redefining it according to the relationships that could enrich it.

Within the scope of the ZIN project, we de-cided to go beyond the notion of energy transition to produce a project that opens up to diverse scales from the micro to the macro, one that is elegant, forward-looking, and contemporary, based on a '*transformation* under strong ecological constraint.' Transition by design, following the example of what is usually called 'research by design,' ena-bles the Transformation Project to be the vehicle for the construction of increasingly hybrid, inter-personal worlds conducive to the coexistence of a variety of different environments, including the workplace, housing, hotels, shops, sports, and leisure activities.

We have attained a biology of the building that has enabled us to naturally address ambitious environmental issues while at the same time offer-ing a renewed spatial framework for enriched practices in a capital city. The large size of the building, the fluidity of its interior passages, the renewed relationship with the city, the transfor-mability and scalability of the building, the energy exchanges that the different programs can effect with one another, and the new place given to nature—in the public greenhouse, on the roof, or as a source of comfort in the new workspaces—are so many conditions that will contribute to the building's robustness over time and ensure that it is part of a solidarity-based and circular future.

DISCREET BUT DIVERSE

In the same way as Toyo Ito describes the mysterious nature of Tokyo as a city without an exterior, an interior labyrinth into which one inadvertently enters at several points, we wanted to make ZIN a building devoid of overwhelming visibility; a building that is unobtrusive and yet present in that it bears witness to a reality that is already there, that does not shrink into the gray expanse of the Brussels metropolis. We did not strive for a great form or a grand composition, but instead respect for what it was. A form of delicacy for what is there, one that does not shy away from what exists but rather imbues it with a new future. It is also a form of frugality in the means used; the architecture is direct, it avoids adding confusion and profusion to territories that are currently overly dominated by signs. In addition to this discretion, we wanted an open architecture that places freedom and diversity at the heart of its issues. It is also a climatic architecture, in the sense that it produces welcoming, stimulating, and often resilient atmospheres. It becomes an architecture for Living, for inhabiting the world, for bringing out the real, the potential for transformation.

IS THE MODERN BRUSSELS PROJECT BEING ACCOMPLISHED OR IS AN ALTER *BRUXELLISATION* AT WORK?

The Northern Quarter project in Brussels, known as 'Manhattan,' contributed to the coinage of the neologism 'bruxellisation' that first emerged in the 1970s, the symptoms of which having already begun to appear in the late 1960s in the wake of the 1958 World's Fair held in Brussels. At that time, the major works in Brussels began, namely the construction of a large European metropolis that was determined to modernize the city in every way possible (increased tertiarization, adaptation of the city to cars through the creation of major

We did not strive for a great form or a grand composition, but instead respect for what it was. A form of delicacy for what is there, one that does not shy away from what exists but rather imbues it with a new future. It is also a form of frugality in the means used; the architecture is direct, it avoids adding confusion and profusion to territories that are currently overly dominated by signs.

infrastructures and tunnels that are still present in today's Brussels, etc.), despite the existence of working-class neighborhoods scheduled for demolition to make way for the modern metropolis.

This historical episode in the recent urban history of Brussels has left many scars: it probably explains why the northern quarters have remained absent from the representations of the city until today. Like other neighborhoods in Brussels, they were the scene of urban resistance, which resulted in the incompletion of a modern project for the northern neighborhoods.

One wonders whether the present sequence represents the completion of the unfinished modern project or whether an alternative *bruxellisation* is taking place, giving this chaotic city a singular future stemming from its eventful architectural and urban history.

Another coincidence? Or is it a random coincidence that this project is located here, on the site of an unforgettable history that is no longer remembered?

Koenraad Van Cleempoel

Rereading[1] WTC: Memory, Trauma, and Shifting Meanings

1. I borrow this concept from Paul Ricœur's *Architecture et narrativité* (1998, trans. 2016). In the book, he explores the relation between the architectural project (inscribed in stone) and literary narrativity (inscribed in language). He develops three steps: *mimesis*, *prefiguration*, and *refiguration*. Ricœur refers to this final step as an act of 'rereading.' This opens rich associations when applied to the theory of adaptive reuse.

2. In 2017 refurbishment accounted for 59 per cent of work in Europe compared with 41 per cent for new builds (https://www.ace-cae.eu/fileadmin/New_Upload/7._Publications/Sector_Study/2016/2016_EN_FN_070217_new.pdf : section 2.3).

3. Plevoets & Van Cleempoel (2019), *Adaptive Reuse of the Built Heritage*, 120–25.

4. Dousset (2011), *Making a City with Words*, quoted in Van De Weijer (2019).

A DISCOURSE OF ADAPTIVE REUSE?

Blank-sheet architecture is increasingly being replaced by attitudes and strategies of adaptive reuse. Recent surveys of the architectural market in Europe show how the architect's work is weighted toward refurbishment.[2] The challenge, however, seems to be on a more qualitative and conceptual level: How to deal intelligently and sustainably with the legacy of previous generations and ideologies? How to create a smart synthesis between the urban and spatial possibilities of a site and contemporary expectations and aspirations? Although the discipline of architecture—both in practice and theory—has been well equipped to handle these situations for centuries, there seem to be new challenges ahead, on the level of both scale and urban narrative.

This essay deals with one of these challenges: can we link the emerging discourse on adaptive reuse to the current transformation of the World Trade Center (WTC) in Brussels, completed in 1967 and remodeled in 2019? We want to reflect on the possibilities of associating a growing field of architectural theory to the WTC and its unprecedented scale to reuse a very specific urban legacy of a generation ago. A legacy that comes with the unsolved expectation of an extreme *tabula rasa* approach and the erasure of the *memory* of a rich urban tissue in Brussels. Handling these immaterial values, in addition to the physical intervention, is one of the parameters, as we will argue below, that brings the redesign of the WTC into the arena of adaptive reuse theory. Paul Ricœur speaks in this sense of continuity and discontinuity:

> Indeed, we might say that a narrative will transform an initial situation into a terminal situation through episodes. There, a dialectic comes into play—of which we will see shortly the interesting parallelism with building—between the discontinuity of something that happens suddenly, and the continuity of the story that goes on through this discontinuity (2016, 35).

It is not so much about completeness or finding definitive solutions, we argue, as about the dynamic concept of transformation as a guiding principle.

Of course, rethinking existing sites and urban situations is not new to the discipline of architecture. Its history is full of examples of the already built being absorbed into new structures, intelligent urban ensembles, private or public spaces. Michelangelo's design of 1563 integrating a church into the ruins of the antique Roman baths of Diocletian (built from 298 to 306) is just one of many examples of how a historical reservoir offers sudden possibilities and potentials after centuries of quiet existence.[3] The scale and language of urban interventions following modernism, however, were extreme, leading to bold statements in relation to existing structures and fabrics presenting urbanists, owners, city councils, and users with unprecedented challenges to give new life to many of these sites a generation later. As their design was focused in an extreme way to serve one purpose only, they now struggle to adapt themselves to new programs that are typically more hybrid. Breaking up this monofunctional approach and strong separation of different functions over different buildings is an obvious but complex design brief.

The question we are interested in is: how can such a 'functional city' be re-urbanized and refocused using the instruments and discourses of adaptive reuse? In the case of the WTC, this challenge is even more complex, because it also needs to address the trauma of destroying its preexisting urban footprint in the 1960s in the process of *bruxellisation* and the ensuing displacement of people.[4] Bringing back the perspective of history, memory and human scale are essential elements to address this question. In his essay 'Initiating Adaptive Reuse of the North Quarter in Brussels,' Marijn Van De Weijer explains rightly that 'there is a reciprocity between heritage and aspects of loss, change and instability. This reciprocity deserves attention in the field of architectural design, as, hypothetically, memories of trauma and displacement might inform the search of a new cycle of usage' (2018, 40).

MEMORY & TRAUMA

If we want link the current reorganization of the WTC to a discourse of adaptive reuse, it is valuable to take into account the notion of 'memory.' In general, the relation between modernism and memory is a difficult one, and this is particularly true for the World Trade Center site. The radical organization of the 'Manhattan Plan' (as it was coined) created a late-modernist high-rise scheme in Brussels finalized in 1967 by the design group Structures. The extreme *tabula rasa* approach of erasing an entire nineteenth-century fabric was combined with an even more extreme ambition and programmatic separation. The 53-hectare modernist plan would consist of some 60 high-rise buildings with open spaces in between and a large motorway acting as a spine to link these 'object buildings.' This scheme was clearly inspired by the organization of the modern city as proposed by Le Corbusier in his *Plan Voisin* (1925) and *Ville Radieuse* (1930).

Such 'functional cities' were based on 'scientifically derived design principles' generating a formula where buildings and transportation were seen as an abstraction of the idea of place, all arranged with a kind of infinite space.[5] A consequence of such a logical and radical approach was the amputation of history: urban expansion, efficiency, and employment became the leading parlance, while historical urban quarters were framed as chaotic, outdated, unhygienic, and malfunctioning.

Criticism of the failure of this modernist ideology on urbanism was wide. The newly built modern cities lacked distinctive historical roots and all cities seemed to look and feel similar.[6] The philosopher Jürgen Habermas captures this tense relation between modernism and memory:

> This explains the rather abstract language in which the modernist temper has spoken of the 'past.' Individual epochs lose their distinct forces. Historical memory is replaced by the heroic affinity of the present with the extremes of history.[7]

The erasure of distinctive historical roots in the Brussels Northern Quarter would thus imply that all memory anchors have disappeared to install a process of reinterpretation of such historical structures. We would therefore like to propose —for the sake of our argument—that both existing towers of 1967 can be considered as monuments or urban artifacts, or even more precisely: a significant imprint. We borrow this concept from Aldo Rossi (1931–1997), who, in his seminal book *The Architecture and the City* (1982), opposes precisely the modern rejection of the past and its memory. Instead, he proposes the idea of history as a kind of framework bearing such an 'imprint' (p. 5). He develops two important concepts also relevant in our considerations on the WTC: that of the 'significant place,' on the one hand, and the semantic separation between history and memory, on the other. First is Rossi's opposition of 'significant place,' in relation to the modernist idea of 'infinite space' flowing through the ordered and zoned city. This lack of orientation and human scale was a clear challenge with WTC and is addressed in the design vision.[8]

More interesting still is how Rossi sees a shift of meaning between history and memory.[9] It goes as follows: History exists if a form maintains its original function. If the form or building has been adapted to a different use, then we are in the realm of memory.[10] This is interesting as it opens up the possibility of considering the adaptation of the WTC as a dynamic process with a focus on *transformation* instead of working from the notion of *completeness.*

In remodeling the WTC—as is also the case with many other adaptive reuse projects—a negotiation between an existing typology and the possibility of a new one emerges. The sole function of office spaces in both towers changes by the gesture of adding a connecting wing between them. This generates an important new spatial configuration: the new 'work floor' has a double height of 5.2 m instead of the regular 2.7 m in the old core towers. The program is extended to a more diverse type of office, combined with living and recreation. A new space for a more diverse working environment.

We can thus consider 'type' here as the frame within which change operates, allowing for a continuous dialectic between the changing program and its users. Rather than being a 'frozen mechanism' to produce architecture, this change of type opens up a continuous negotiation between the past and the future, typical of adaptive reuse projects of a certain scale. Raphael Moneo intreprets this as 'a continuous process of transformation, where the architect can extrapolate from the type, changing its use, he can distort the type by means of a transformation of scale; he can overlap different types to produce new one. He can use formal quotations of a known type in a different context, as well as create new types by a radical change in the techniques already employed. The list of different mechanisms is extensive—it is a function of the inventiveness of architects.'[11] It is precisely when architecture gives up a known type and generates the formula for a new type that an interesting new situation occurs. Moneo continues: 'When a type emerges—when an architect is able to describe a new set of formal relations which generates a new group of buildings or elements—then that architect's contribution has reached the level of generality and anonymity that characterizes architecture as a discipline.'[12] This description seems appropriate for the process of transformation at the WTC: through its urban gesture, an intelligent variation on an extremely formal typology of the office towers emerges and creates new conditions for an alternative meaning. This new link between memory and typology operates equally on the scale of the interior and on the urban level. For the latter, we would like to elaborate the notion of re-urbanization.

A VOCABULARY OF RE-URBANIZATION IN THE ARCHITECTURE OF ADDITIONS

An exhibition at the Architectural Association in London in 1980 based on the work of Rodrigo Pérez de Arce provides relevant concepts in relation to the reuse of the WTC. The title of the exhibition: *Dacca, Chandigarh, Runcorn: Three*

How to deal intelligently and sustainably with the legacy of previous generations and ideologies?
How to create a smart synthesis between the urban and spatial possibilities of a site and contemporary expectations and aspirations?

5. Hale (2000), *Buildings Ideas: An Introduction to Architectural Theory.*
6. Tanghe, Vlaeminck, and Berghoef (1984), *Living Cities: A Case for Urbanism and Guidelines for Re-urbanization*
7. Habermas (2013), 'Modernity: An Incomplete Project,' in Foster (1983), *The Anti-Aesthetic*, p. 5.
8. 'Diversity and adaptability are the core ideas … We focus on two important scales: the scale of the user and the scale of the city … The highway has degenerated into an oversized and introverted space that does not connect to the rest of the city. The Noordwijk today is a bit of a victim of the dominant presence of that space. The base of the WTC is designed to turn away from this space rather than make a relationship with it.' *Zin in Noord: kernnota 3.1 visie meerwaarde architectuur*, 5.12.2018.
9. Rossi aligns with a rich tradition associating architecture with memory— see Whyte (2003); Bastéa (2004).
10. From Marsh's introduction to de Arce's *Urban Transformations* (2015), viii–xxv.
11. Moneo (1978), *On Typology, Oppositions.*
12. Ibid.

13. 'Urban Transformations,' 24 April–16 May 1980. The Architectural Association, 34–36 Bedford Square, London WC1. (De Arce, 2015, 37.)
14. Machado (1976), *Old Buildings as Palimpsests.* 49.
15. J. Malpas (2012), *Building Memory.*

Projects for the Re-urbanization of the Modern City. De Arce is a Chilean architect who graduated from AA with a conceptual thesis on re-urbanizing failed modernist sites. His core argument is the need for a city to have an original nucleus that can be transformed. He is critical of the 'bankruptcy of modernist planning' that tried to universalize the city as a mathematical city-machine. And how, then, the 'aura' of 'the building as an individualized object as well as that of the street piazza, court of city-block as particularized places had been disdainfully eradicated.' This creates the setting for the work of de Arce in which the curator of the AA exhibition, Demetri Porphyrios, observes two major issues underlying his work: a concern for the re-urbanization of the *Ville Radieuse* and a concern for the sedimentation of architectural history. In the introduction he notes: 'The project for re-urbanisation of the modernist city embattles the scientific cult of "order without rhetoric."'[13] Similarly, his project for the sedimentation of architectural history aims at a critique of the serialized universality of modernism. Perez de Arce substitutes the lavishness of iconographic association for the sobriety of a factitious utilitarianism, hoping to retrieve in this way the lost 'aura' of architecture.

De Arce himself sees the exhibition with his drawings as an 'intermediate stage in the development of an idea.' It is not conclusive; rather it is an attempt to correctly identify a problem. In this humble fashion, he presents urban possibilities of three sites that deal with the accumulative construction as a relevant 'alternative to fragmentation caused by modern urbanism.' Starting from this fragmentary urban order, his (paper) urban interventions try to generate a new order with 'the original vocabulary.' This design methodology clearly illustrates an experimental attitude and ease in dealing with the site's monumental character. The third project in the exhibition is probably most fitting as a case for our essay on the WTC. Runcorn is an industrial town southeast of Liverpool. In 1964 it was designated as a new town and its population doubled. There were large-scale architectural interventions, including the Southgate Estate, a modernist public housing project designed by James Stirling (1926–1992). Comprising 1,500 residential units to house 6,000 people, it was connected by a pedestrian bridge to a 'shopping city.' When completed in 1977 it was one of the largest covered shopping centers in Europe. Again, de Arce's answer is one of scale, architectural additions, and inserting large gardens:

> The programme for the re-urbanisation of Runcorn includes the reconstruction of the urban blocks, the breaking down of the monolithic shopping center into small units, and diffusing the monumental character of the existing house. A small assembly hall dominates the central area. The fountain square in the heart of the city, in which the colossal viaduct forms of Stirling's project are developed as

a portico serving as a façade for the town. The 'L'-shaped blocks are enclosed, forming perimeter blocks which include small internal court buildings. The roofs are developed into allotment gardens and the new corner buildings emerge as garden pavilions. What will happen to Runcorn and other modern cities we do not know.

Well, sadly, we do know: between 1990 and 1992—ten years after de Arce's exhibition in London—the Southgate Estate was demolished and replaced with another housing development, known as Hallwood Park, based around more traditional design principles. This seems to be the fate of similar modernist ensembles in Europe. They therefore somehow run the risk of falling into the same trap as the *tabula rasa* approach of the modernists before them. The transformation of the WTC is therefore an interesting alternative that tries to start a dialogue with the memory of the city—albeit an unsettled memory.

CONCLUSION: SHIFTING MEANINGS

Often used in the theory of adaptive reuse is the metaphor of the palimpsest, a manuscript or piece of writing material on which later writing has been superimposed on erased earlier writing. In an influential paper of 1976, Rodolfo Machado associated this notion with historical meaning: 'In the process of remodelling the past takes a greater significance because it, itself, is the material to be altered and reshaped. The past provides the already—written, the marked "canvas" on which each successive remodelling will find its own place. Thus, the past becomes a "package of sense," of built-up meaning to be accepted (maintained), transformed, or suppressed (refused).'[14]

At the WTC, this package of sense also relates to the troubled past of destruction and displacement of former inhabitants. Its process of adaptive reuse—and its associated meanings—therefore extends its realm from material to immaterial values. The notion of memory as a corridor between past and future use is valuable, but we need to be aware that in the WTC, it also gives us memories of an unsettled past. We might find a solution in the writings of the American philosopher Jeff Malpas, who elaborates on the triangle between time, space, and memory by introducing the notion of placemaking.[15] For him, architecture is 'as much a *response* to place, a *conversation* with place as it is *making* of place.' His *places* are not static but dynamic, and it is through this performative character that place, memory, and buildings are bound together. This also makes sense in the WTC—and our attempt in this essay to frame its process of transformation in an emerging theory of adaptive reuse—as Malpas continues to argue that 'we should think of buildings, not as inert structures that stand apart from remembrance, from felt experience, sentiment, or affect, but as constituted romantically and materially at one and the same time. In terms of memory, buildings carry

Koenraad Van Cleempoel

Rereading WTC

memory as an essential and inevitable part of what they are, and they do this in several ways.'

To control this process, he refers to narrative as a vehicle: how every narrative is embedded in that which it also aims to narrate. To what extent does the story belong to the material and the material to the story? The construction of a sustainable narrative that balances a given typology and its associated historical meaning, on the one hand, and a new program in a transformed type, is what emerges at the WTC. And the architect's narrative does exactly that by explaining how 'circular thinking changes the way you design architecture. Due to the large dimensions [of the WTC], the use can evolve in the future: the renewed project is robust over time, because of its structure and dimensions, because of the various circulation possibilities and because of its relationship with the city. The introduction of greenery also makes it a healthy and attractive as destination. This diversity of conditions makes the building a barrel of possibilities for an open and circular future.'[16]

16. Press release, 12 March 2019. *Brussels North: Innovative Reuse of the Iconic WTC Project Sets New Standards for Circular Construction.*

REFERENCES

Bastéa, E. (ed.) (2004). *Memory and Architecture*, Albuquerque: University of New Mexico Press.

de Arce, R. P. (2015). 'Urban Transformations and the Architecture of Additions.' Introduction by Julian March. In: H. Meller (ed.). *Studies in International Planning History*. London; New York: Routledge.

Dousset, I. (2011). 'Making a City with Words: Understanding Brussels through Its Urban Heroes and Villains.' *City, Culture and Society*, 3(2), 105–116.

Hale, J. (2000). *Building Ideas: An Introduction to Architectural Theory*. Chichester: Wiley and Sons.

Malpas, J. (2012). 'Building Memory.' *Interstices: Journal of Architecture and Related Arts*, 13.

Moneo, R. (1978). 'On Typology.' *Oppositions: A Journal for Ideas and Criticism in Architecture*. Published for the Institute for Architecture and Urban Studies by MIT Press.

Mumford, E. P. (2002). *The CIAM Discourse on Urbanism, 1928–1960*. Cambridge, Mass.: MIT Press.

Van Cleempoel, K. (2018). 'A Short Note on Traces and Memory.' In: K. Van Cleempoel (ed.), *Trace n° 1: On Tradition; Notes on Adaptive Reuse*. Hasselt, 2018.

Van De Wijer, M. (2018). 'Traces of Trauma: Initiating Adaptive Reuse of the North Quarter in Brussels.' In: K. Van Cleempoel (ed.), *Trace n° 1: On Tradition; Notes on Adaptive Reuse*. Hasselt, 2018.

Heynen, H., & A. Loeckx (1998). 'Scenes of Ambivalence: Concluding Remarks on Architectural Patterns of Displacement.' *Journal of Architectural Education*, 52(2).

Smith, L. (2006). *Uses of Heritage*. London; New York: Routledge.

Ricœur, P. (1998). 'Architecture et narrativité.' *Urbanisme*, no. 303, November–December, 44–51. Translated and republished (2016) as 'Architecture and Narrativity.' *Études Ricœuriennes / Ricœur Studies*, 7(2), 31–42.

Rossi, A. (1982). *The Architecture of the City*. Cambridge, Mass.: MIT Press.

Tanghe, J., S. Vlaeminck & J. Berghoef (1984). *Living Cities: A Case for Urbanism and Guidelines for Re-urbanization*. Oxford: Pergamon Press.

Whyte, I. B. (ed.) (2003). *Modernism and the Spirit of the City*. London: Routledge.

Jan de Moffarts, 'The Forgotten History of the Northern Quarter,' unpublished paper, June 2018.

'The lack of any human scale and of pleasant, quality places to stay is due, on the one hand, to the abandonment of the spatial elements, relationships and principles of the design. On the other hand, it is due to the megalomaniacal design. The totalitarian approach and excessively rigid plan are in part responsible for the failure of the Manhattan Plan.'

Jan de Moffarts

Kristiaan Borret, Brussels Government Architect

Transcript of a conversation that took place at perspective.brussels in November 2018 in the framework of research for a thesis within the LSE Cities Programme.

  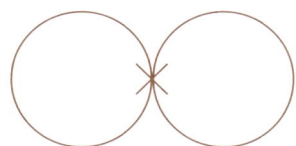

Interview by Dieter Leyssen

DL Dieter Leyssen
KB Kristiaan Borret

INTRODUCTION: TEMPORARY USE IN THE SWING BETWEEN BOTTOM-UP AND TOP-DOWN

DL Michael Guggenheim wrote in 2014 that in the second half of the twentieth century, the driving force behind projects for reuse was constantly shifting between the user, the architect, and society. Jane Jacobs took the initiative away from the architect and gave it to the user. Postmodernism returned the authority to the architect. In the last decade, following the property crisis of 2008, temporary use and reuse has become extremely popular and in many cases is an instrument for branding and place-making. If we take the example of the Northern Quarter in Brussels, where do you think the driving force in this experiment lies? How can the public authorities deal with this evolution?

KB I first wish to react to your initial statement that developers deploy temporary use for placemaking. If you take a broad view, we know that the origin of temporary use lies in alternative bottom-up circles and not in established professional circles such as the development sector or the public authorities. It served as a kind of countermovement or form of activism. But today you can indeed see that others are taking over the practice. Developers do it for place-making and branding purposes in order to attract future apartment buyers. This temporary activity is therefore essentially commercial. I recall Project 2 in Antwerp,[1] a hip cocktail bar that mainly attracted people from Brasschaat and other suburbs.[2] This is to be found in all genres. The government does it too, and to a certain extent I don't think there's anything wrong with it. I am not ashamed to say that the government should instrumentalize temporary use—on the condition that it's taken seriously and that temporary use is seen as a way of, for example, finding programs that are useful and work well in that location or were unexpected, or to test out something we have in mind. In this way, temporary use becomes a test phase. Let me give a simple example. A skate park is going to be created in the new park at Vergote Dock in Brussels because it turned out that the skating events organized by Toestand are very popular;[3] there is a public for that type of activity in the neighborhood (even if said public doesn't buy apartments); the program is at home in that location. So this is a good example of the fact that temporary use is not just something that can be discarded once place-making has been achieved, but something that has an effect on the realization of the 'permanent' program for the location. In such a way, temporary use fits into a more systematic urban-planning approach that one could call transition urbanism.

DL In that particular example, are the initiators of the temporary use still involved in the permanent program?

1. Kristiaan Borret was Antwerp's city architect from 2006 to 2014.
2. Brasschaat is a well-off suburb of Antwerp.
3. Toestand is a Brussels NGO responsible for the temporary 'Allée du Kaai' program of events at Vergote Dock.
4. Brussels Instituut voor Milieubeheer (Brussels Institute for Environmental Management).
5. The autonomous municipal agency responsible for project development on public land.

KB   No, only the program remains. The authorities are building the new skate park on the same site, and we are assuming that it will be used by the same users and new ones. It will be run by the staff managing the new park. I think that's logical. In the long term, you can't leave the management to organizations involved in temporary use. The result is that Toestand has to move. It would be wrong to have them in the same place forever. That is the nature of that type of organization, and they share that point of view.

     To return to your first question, I like to encourage a model where the authorities play a part in facilitating and accommodating bottom-up initiatives. I believe it's possible to have a sort of swinging movement whereby the authorities systematically enable and provide support for temporary activities. In my view, the best example is Parckfarm. It is always presented as a bottom-up case, but it is not. It is just as much top-down. There was a grant from the BIM,[4] a competition also organized by the BIM, and a tendering process. I believe strongly in this swinging between top-down and bottom-up. In Antwerp at the time I was in favor of AG Vespa no longer building everything itself,[5] but rather providing support for new citizen projects such as co-housing. At present, people who want to engage in co-housing always miss the boat because by the time the whole group has agreed to buy something, a project developer will often have gotten hold of the site. The authorities could put plots on the market that are intended solely for co-housing. The tendering procedures could then be made long enough to give everyone time to amass the sum needed for their bid. What you do in this way is to make private self-building or housing groups possible on land owned by the local authority. In this way, the city council voluntarily lets go of the land without itself building, but does influence the market so that groups like this are given a chance. In doing so, one is activating things both top-down and bottom-up. I think that's marvelous. The authorities can't do everything themselves, but neither can everything be done bottom-up. But there is a role for the authorities in which they remain 'the authorities' and actually provide the framework for and facilitate this bottom-up approach. The swing between top-down and bottom-up is in my view important for contemporary urban planning. I believe in the paradox that a neighborhood initiative can emerge thanks to the authorities because they offered a framework for it or provided a financial catalyst.

DL   How does one detect the most effective points in the program for temporary use in order to extend them into permanent use? Are there other things that can be tested by means of temporary use and, if so, how are they found?

KB   If you reflect on how you can anchor this swing (between bottom-up and top-down) structurally, you might, for example, think of including in the tendering process for temporary users a clause saying that an evaluation will be made after three years, on which basis the possibility of further development may be offered—a sort of analysis report. This is different from temporary use as a form of activism, where a lot happens on the basis of 'gut feeling' without much self-reflection. If you organize it in a swinging movement, you can link it to a process of reflection that brings lessons to the surface. You could also put forward objectives and goals, for instance on the level of social impact. What is found to be positive is of course a value judgment. The developer may think it's excellent that lots of young people from Brasschaat have been to his cocktail bar, while it may have had little significance for local anchoring.

DL   In projects on the scale of the Northern Quarter, isn't there more of a triangle than a swing: the developer/investor, the authorities, and thirdly, the users?

KB   The Northern Quarter is certainly a specific case because there are so many private interests involved. The authorities are more on the sidelines because the area was not acknowledged in the beginning as a strategic program from a traditional planning perspective. In that instance, the question is more what the developer will get out of the temporary use. As the Bouwmeester (Brussels government architect), I was only able to get myself involved by means of private redevelopment projects.

DL   But you are ultimately the regulator, aren't you?

KB   That's right. It is my strong belief that in the end, the public authorities should regulate in view of the public interest, even if that might sound a bit old-fashioned. But at the moment, we have little influence on the choice of programs in the Northern Quarter. The government was not involving itself closely in the beginning.

DL   Let's zoom out for a moment to view the bigger picture. The Northern Quarter in Brussels is about to undergo change. This means added value can be generated, both social and financial. Various urban issues may come up. Such initiatives as LabNorth highlight the need for affordable workspaces by temporarily providing room for various small-scale initiatives —initially only temporarily, but with an eye to a more permanent supply and demand. On which other fronts can success be achieved? And, as the Bouwmeester, how do you plan to contribute?

6.   Plan d'Aménagement Directeur (master plan).
7.   Zone d'Entreprises en Milieu Urbain (industrial estates in the urban environment).

KB   In a sense, temporary use could be like scientific research: you start with a hypothesis and then test it out. In the Northern Quarter, the hypothesis was that it might well be possible one day to fill the office buildings in the area with lots of small-scale users. There was no prior evidence for this. You didn't know whether there would be enough small users or whether they would want to be in the Northern Quarter. This hypothesis was tested by an initial call for candidates, and at first sight it appeared to be correct: a great many organizations applied. In my view, the second question is whether a developer would be happy with this in the long term. If, considering the current crisis (i.e., the overabundant supply of office space), they are happy with it, it's better than nothing. But would they also see it as a model for the future? It's not a doing-by-learning process, but learning-by-doing. By doing it, one understands better and minds change. This is also why we, Team Bouwmeester, rather than come up with high-minded visions on the long term, we prefer to work in the Brussels situation on real projects because of their short-term impact. Basing them on a pragmatic vision, however, they could function as catalyst or pilot projects and thus have influence beyond the project itself. For the Northern Quarter, we start from the manifest necessity that the area should be more mixed functionally. In terms of spatial structure, we try to turn the main axis of the district into the direction of Boulevard Simon Bolivar and thus better connect it with the canal on the one hand and the slope of Schaerbeek on the other. We try systematically to push this idea with every project we supervise. In this way we want to gradually realize a general transformation of the Northern Quarter.

DL   By 'doing' in a particular project you can really learn quickly and draw conclusions. In a sense, this contradicts the more traditional planning approach. Time is needed to anchor the lessons learned from temporary use in structural policy. For an investor, economic preconditions can soon change, bringing the risk that certain programs that seemed to work suddenly become outdated. The Bouwmeester acts as an intermediary between these two realities. How do you deal with these different speeds?

KB   It's true that the Bouwmeester has a pivotal, overlapping, intermediary function between different speeds or different circles. Because the Team Bouwmeester is transversal—at home in both places—and knows something of both property matters and public planning, it can engage in transfers of knowledge and at the same time keep up to date on what's happening on both sides. I have countless examples of what we call the 'free benefit'; you obtain this as a Bouwmeester simply because you are in several places at the same time. In addition, it also comes from developing a sensitivity. It's a little like what Bernardo Secchi used to say when the structural plan for Antwerp was being drawn up: there is top-down and bottom-up. The very minor concrete things that happen can be extrapolated to a more general plan that becomes credible because you have at any rate had one test case. So it comes down to extrapolating test cases and, in the reverse direction, engaging in the generation of a theoretical plan. LabNorth's hypothesis is the development of affordable workspaces for various small organizations; my hypothesis as Bouwmeester is that it should be possible to have housing in the Northern Quarter. My guess is that, with the added value that housing is currently yielding and the area's strategic location, the market is capable at the moment of absorbing relatively cheap 'pioneer dwellings.' This is a hypothesis that was conceived top-down and it therefore comes down to repeating it in various circles, until someone takes the bait and is willing to develop a test case.

DL   In the long term too, the government is able to determine what percentage achieves a good balance for both affordable workplaces and the housing stock. It might be decided, for example, that 30 per cent affordable workplaces and 20 per cent housing in the Northern Quarter is best. Do you support that kind of regulation?

The very minor concrete things that happen can be extrapolated to a more general plan that becomes credible because you have at any rate had one test case. So it comes down to extrapolating test cases and, in the reverse direction, engaging in the generation of a theoretical plan.

DL   Dieter Leyssen
KB   Kristiaan Borret

KB   I think you could do that. Imagine that in time we will evolve toward a PAD,[6] whereby you lay down a zoning plan. A zoning plan cannot be underestimated as a tool of spatial planning because it determines the value of the land. In my view, the best proof lies in the ZEMUs,[7] zones for new residential development, where the authorities have stipulated that a minimum proportion of production activity should be maintained. Without these regulations, this production would no longer be there, because the land value in these zones has become that of residential land. In this way you can secure their diverse nature. The plan for the Northern Quarter should be an evolution toward a better mix, not monofunctional offices. This means that we should impose a minimal presence of housing and amenities. I believe that we shall evolve toward that sort of regulation for the Northern Quarter.

But as a government body you often play a double role. Firstly that of regulator, writing the regulations for others. But we ourselves are often the landowner. For example, the Canal Plan arose partly as a result of regulation (master plan, ZEMUs) and partly by developing its own land differently. It will be the same with the Northern Quarter. The Brussels-Capital Region owns a large share of the CCN building next to the Brussels-North station. So if this building were to be put on the market, we will also have to think about the level of mix we want. As an owner we are faced with the choice of acting in an exemplary way by ourselves, generating an interesting test case, versus selling the piece of land for only the greatest possible profit.

MIXED USE, DIVERSITY, AND URBAN LIFE

DL   A mixed program was also put forward when the development of the Northern Quarter began in the 1960s. But, because at the time offices were the most profitable form of property, it became a monofunctional office area. Nowadays the notion of mixed use is back on the table. Temporary use, which aims for more mixed use, is a practice that was not implemented 50 years ago. So, for example, there is a school, a new café, and in the spring a major exhibition will form part of the temporary use of WTC I. It's to be hoped that these functions will then be translated into a long-term plan. A more fundamental argument is to be made, which is that mixed use is characteristic of urban life and an urban society functions on the basis of difference. Over the last few decades, the Northern Quarter has mainly accommodated commuters who used the area from nine to five and took very little responsibility for it. By introducing differences and the conflicts that go with them, a different sort of citizenship may arise.

KB   Mixed use is good, and not only because it introduces 24-hour use and thereby also generates social safety. Really in a fundamental way I see mixed use as an essential characteristic of urban life. The more practical question that remains in the Northern Quarter is on which scale. It does not mean, for example, that every building has to be completely mixed. So in the encouragement of mixed use one also has to think of variety: a varied range of spaces for housing and work. This is an essential characteristic of urban life and we should want to see it all over the city.

When it comes to housing, things are more complex since it is a category in planning legislation that covers a lot. It includes hotels, expat homes, short-stay homes, long-stay flats, and of course privately owned individual flats. The latter usually lead to greater anchoring in the neighborhood because these owners appropriate their environment more. I am currently arguing very vigorously to separate part of the housing stock to make it available for sale as individual flats, because I assume that someone who buys will be more likely to engage in the neighborhood and invest in it too. If a paving stone is loose, they will be the ones to call the relevant department to have it seen to. They really care about their neighborhood in the long term.

> DL   At the same time, lots of dwellings are being bought by small investors who then let them. The promised prices are not always obtained, which once again leads to vacant properties. The UpSite tower is a good example.

KB   It's true that that is a risk. My feeling is that at some point there will be enough demand for small starter homes for sale in the Northern Quarter, and I really hope that there will be enough people buying in order to go and live there themselves.

The variety of users is in any case important for the appropriation of the district. For example, it is currently impossible to have a neighborhood committee in the Northern Quarter because there are simply no inhabitants. If a few hotels and short-stay flats appear, there still won't be a committee. It will only appear when there are inhabitants who truly see the area as their home.

FROM TRAUMA TO THE DEVELOPMENT OF THE DISCIPLINE

> DL   The Northern Quarter is a major trauma in the history of Brussels urban planning. How do you, as Bouwmeester, deal with that?

KB   There is indeed a trauma. I feel like I belong to some kind of in-between generation. The generation before me experienced the demolition of the district and still hasn't digested the brutalities of the big shots who were responsible for it. As I see it, that's a less emotional trauma of that kind of late-modernist architecture that turns its back on the city. That is my trauma and that of my generation—buildings that have nothing to do with the city. The KBC offices on Materialenkaai are in that respect the same as the WTC—architecture that does not engage with the city. I absolutely want to repair and remedy this kind of urban failure. And then there is also the heritage trauma: so much heritage has been demolished in Brussels, from both the eighteenth and nineteenth centuries. Let's not make the same mistake now by demolishing twentieth-century heritage. As you can see, there is more than one trauma in the Northern Quarter. There is the trauma of the inhabitants who were forced out, the trauma of the modernist buildings that do not enter into any relations with the city, and then there is the trauma of 'aren't we making the same mistake?'

> DL   That trauma was evident in the talk by ARAU in the recent debate entitled 'Should I Stay or Should I Go.'[8] But it seems that this trauma is still very much alive in Brussels and is also having an impact on younger generations.

KB   I don't think so. Many young people are fascinated by the aesthetics of the late-modernist office developments. Two crystalline towers, corporate arcadias—I know younger people who do not reject this architecture. I feel that in my generation there is this sense that a moment of revenge has come. There is this feeling that we can now correct what the earlier generation of policymakers and developers built. But while ARAU appear to be arguing more for a return to the original premodern state, for me it's more a matter of 'making some good contemporary city now.' By the way, not all of these modern interventions in the urban fabric were completely badly done. I have always criticized Renaat Braem's beautiful police tower in Antwerp for the very bad way it touches the ground and fits between the neighboring buildings. Whereas, for example, the more banal Antwerp tower on Keyserlei is much less disruptive in its context because it has a lower plinth of shops and bars that stimulates urban life around it. In that sense, fine and ugly architecture and good and bad integration into the city are not always the same.

> DL   By comparison with the Antwerp tower, the Monnaie and Philips buildings here in Brussels are also being redeveloped.

8. L'Atelier de Recherche et d'Action Urbaines (Atelier for research and urban action) is an NGO founded in 1969. In his role as Bouwmeester, on 25 October 2017, Kristiaan Borret organized the debate in the Phillips building (another example of a late-modernist office building) on the involvement of architects, policymakers and developers in the redevelopment of this sort of building.

DL   Dieter Leyssen
KB   Kristiaan Borret

KB   Architecturally, the Philips tower has a well-crafted plinth design, but it worked very badly in urban-planning terms. Whereas the new plinth of the Monnaie building, which is awfully generic, actually works well now. All the entrances that were previously oriented inward within a kind of shopping mall typology are now directed toward the pavement and therefore do the right thing by activating the primary public space of the city center.

DL   We learn from such cities as Paris and London, and Berlin too, that it is becoming difficult for small-scale creative and social practices to rent a central location. These are the sorts of organizations that create a great deal of value in the course of urban development but who find that it does not flow back to them afterward. Is there any way of anticipating and dealing with this?

KB   We can see the same thing in the Canal Zone in Brussels. Its success means there are more and more housing projects that reinforce the displacement of other activities. What the authorities should do is set the dynamic in motion and then keep it in check. The latter is much more difficult than the former. In my view, the classic response is once again to set minimum thresholds. At a certain moment we shall have to impose a 10 per cent minimum of social housing in the canal zone. I also argue regularly for buildings for social workspaces or office space. We subsidize housing for people who cannot afford to live in the city because we consider diversity important for the city. But in fact the same thing should apply to businesses and offices. At some point we should put up office or workshop buildings that are subsidized so that companies can rent them in accordance with a number of criteria. It's already happening for start-ups.

DL   This evolution would also have an impact on the typology of an office building. An architectural firm or college has different expectations from the average multinational. The Sint-Lucas studio on the 24th floor of the WTC works perfectly in a worn-out office space.

KB   Is that entirely true? I don't believe it's the perfect place for a school.

DL   In any case, the location works well as an intellectual stimulus for the students. One of the students said that he had never spent so much time in a place with a panoramic view of the city. In this way, the college creates the possibility of a more democratic use of a previously exclusive typology.

KB   There you're right, that's true. The location of the WTC is indeed stimulating, perhaps in a comparable way as it was once thrilling to have a studio in a derelict industrial building of the early twentieth century. It was cold, it echoed too much, and it was not so practical for courses but one was enchanted by the value in that utilitarian architecture. The (sometimes even ominous) charm of a former industrial area was totally different from a normal school environment. In short, it is the tempting force of heterotopia, being in another environment with other rules and standards. What a wonderfully ironic revenge! Who could expect that a late-modernist real-estate operation of brutal capitalism would now be praised as an inspiring environment for young people's education?

SOURCES

Doucet, Isabelle. *The Practice Turn in Architecture: Brussels after 1968*. Ashgate: New York, 2015.

Guggenheim, Michael. 'From Prototyping to Allotyping.' *Journal of Cultural Economy*, 7(4), 2014, pp. 411–433.

Isabelle Doucet, 'An Interview at the WTC Brussels: Architectural Practice and Education "From the Inside Out,"' in 'Schools & Teachers: The Education of an Architect in Europe,' special issue, *Oase*, no. 102, March 2019, pp. 94–104.

'Urban activism in the 1970s in Brussels was mainly known for the campaigns of Noordwijk and ARAU. At the time, the destructive nature of spatial planning called an oppositional activism into being that was expressly against established planning and against the developers, both in Brussels and elsewhere. And yet, this kind of activism is often eventually, unintentionally, encapsulated, and in some cases even results in exactly the kind of architecture it originally opposed. It seems to me that the approach taken today, at the WTC, works "from the inside out": the developer is tolerated as a stakeholder. But a critical practice "from the inside out" does not come without its pitfalls.'

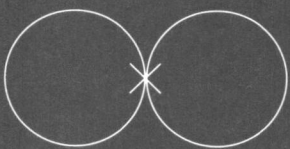

Isabelle Doucet

22

Karine Dana

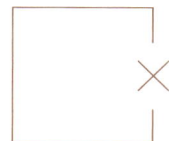

Filming Chance

VIDEOS

The six videos resulting from
these situations are accessible
on the subARCHITECTURE
channel (https://vimeo.com
/channels/subarchitecture).

WTC TEMPORARY
OCCUPATION
https://vimeo.com
/484046997

MULTIPLICITY: 51N4E
with LabNorth in Brussels
https://vimeo.com
/265887566

WTC ARCHITECTURAL
COMPETITION

   Movies, Part 1

WTC_ACT_1: Smart Ways
of Working
https://vimeo.com/329116070
WTC_ACT_2: Making City
https://vimeo.com/329121368
WTC_ACT_3: Living Together
https://vimeo.com/329125666

   Movies, Part 2

WTC_Living_Collage:
https://vimeo.com/329154568

My involvement in the chain of events that took place at the WTC began both spontaneously and unexpectedly. Following a casual meeting with Freek and Johan about the possibility of making films about their work, I began shooting the situation of absolute uncertainty in which they found themselves in August 2017, just after their 'wild' move into the 16th floor of the WTC I tower. I was interested in the idea of filming a process, a reality in a state of transformation, and not a result or any kind of achievement. I then began to work that day with the idea of producing 'shreds' of films … Between August 2017 and December 2018, I came and shot several times the evolution of the spaces, the relations, the behaviors of the occupants of this tower whose number and activity were systematically growing. Beyond the future project, whose design was beginning to take shape, a real, living, and vital process was under way on the floors. It called for energies and connections of all kinds with micro-programs that gradually took shape around the initiators of this open dynamic, for instance, 51N4E, Up4North, AWB, and Vraiment Vraiment. A library here, a school there, as well as a canteen and various associations progressively joined the project, making it possible for the role of the architect to be decentered.

How was I to approach and shoot these gaps, these superpositions, these simultaneities? This was the main question I asked myself throughout the shooting. The camera was used here as an active and indispensable tool in unique social, architectural, and cultural experiences, offering several ways of entering the transformation project of the Northern Quarter of Brussels.

Alessandro Gess

Challenging Real Estate

Notes on the Architectural Transformation of the Brussels World Trade Center

For all those involved, the project for the transformation of the Brussels World Trade Center has been an extraordinary journey. In retrospect, it seems clear that the singularity of the urban situation in the Northern Quarter, combined with the complexity of the task required for a new kind of design approach, proved capable of bridging disciplines and forming new alliances. The work on the architectural design, which took place in the shared project atelier on-site, managed to established a form of learning environment, creating a momentum and opportunity to collectively produce change. This note is an attempt to retrace how things came together.

DEMOLITION VS. TRANSFORMATION

Over the past decade, various projects attempted to propose a conclusive scenario for the future of WTC I and II in the Northern Quarter. Most projects consisted in the demolition of the existing towers, freeing up room for a new real-estate development, but for various reasons none of those projects managed to produce a viable solution. As a direct consequence of those failed redevelopment attempts, the stakeholders, and in particular Befimmo as the principal owner, gradually began to shift away from the idea of demolishing the buildings and began considering the possibility of transforming the existing structure. It is in this context that 51N4E and l'AUC were selected in 2017 to participate in the architectural competition, jointly organized by the owner and the Brussels Bouwmeester (government architect). The priorities of both parties were different—complementary, one could argue. Befimmo's main intention was to anticipate the departure of the tenant occupying WTC II and to envision the transformation of an obsolete part of their property portfolio in order to adapt to the current and future expectations of the commercial

real-estate market. The interests of the city mainly lay in the opportunity to introduce mixed use into the Northern Quarter and to articulate its transformation with the development of the Canal Plan. The project alliance combining the owner and the Brussels Bouwmeester in the very early stages of the project definition was relatively new in the Brussels context and unprecedented in a project of that scale.

THE BUILDING AS TEST SITE

The vacancy of large parts of WTC I opened up the possibility for a temporary occupation, which would become a powerful and vibrant experiment, challenging the programmatic future of the building from within. The project atelier on the 15th floor would become the central point for the development of the project, making it possible to experiment with the future architecture of the building while occupying it. Many ideas and concepts were developed using the building as a programmatic, spatial, and technical real-scale model. During this phase, we as planners were able to experiment with ideas and technical solutions which directly influenced the design of the project, such as the natural ventilation of the façade (on the 23rd floor, the installation of a large sliding window allowed us to experiment with natural ventilation strategies for the façade), the introduction of public spaces in the building (the roof garden on the plinth made it possible to anticipate the future greenhouse on the southeast corner of the plot), and so on. Thanks to these opportunities, the on-site atelier became a prolific learning environment, creating bridges between the past, present, and future of the World Trade Center and the Northern Quarter.

CHALLENGING STANDARDS, NORMS, AND PROGRAMMATIC SPECIALIZATION

From a spatial point of view, our design attempted to tackle three main points.

1. How to transform typical floors into capable and flexible spaces

We understood the transformation as an opportunity to challenge the typical codes and standards of commercial real estate by introducing a diversity of spatial situations rather than one unique optimized spatial configuration. To compensate the relatively low floor-to-floor height of 3.2 m in the existing building, we proposed to connect both towers (WTC I and II) with a new building consisting of 14 double-height spaces spanning from core to core, each forming what we would nickname a 'Volume Capable' (capable space). Each of these Volumes Capables measured roughly 100 m in length, 23 m in width, and 6.5 m in height (typical floor section). With the introduction of the Volume Capable strategy, we attempted to challenge the repetitiveness of the typical office floors of the WTC, creating more spatial diversity, allowing for flexibility and adaptability to change over time. The spatial generosity of the Volumes Capables made it possible to imagine

The zebra scheme is undoubtedly one of the best examples of how the design process managed to challenge fundamental certainties of the commercial real-estate market by introducing a smart and truly hand-tailored solution for a problem.

new forms of configurations of the office spaces and to introduce a specific interior landscape and plantation strategy throughout the building. Free of any vertical circulation or technical installation, the plan of the Volume Capable offered endless possibilities to organize work environments, creating a multiplicity of architectural situations.

As a result of the connection of both towers, the new typical plan constituted continuous plateaus of roughly 5,000 square meters per floor (combining single-height office floors around the existing cores and the double-height space of the central Volume Capable). This new spatial configuration, which contained larger floors on fewer levels, relied entirely on the existing vertical circulations of the two cores. By reducing the number of typical floors from 28 (in the existing WTC) to 14 in the future building, we improved the efficiency of the vertical circulation of the building, reducing the number of elevator stops of the office floors. The spatial and architectural reorganization made it possible to combine the efficiency of vertical circulation in low-rise buildings with the metropolitan qualities and views in high-rise buildings. The proportion of the Volume Capable and its spacious structural grid, which reuses almost exclusively the existing foundations of the WTC, made it possible to imagine a future adaptability or transformation of the building into laboratories or educational facilities.

2. How to introduce mixed use

The mixed-use program of the project (offices, hotel, apartments), combined with the ambition to reuse the two existing building cores as shared vertical infrastructures (elevators, stairs, shafts, etc.), required a spatial solution allowing for each program to have access independently to the core without creating conflicts in use. To solve this, we proposed to elevate the office lobby and its access to the core on the first floor of the Volume Capable. This resulted in the creation of a direct access for the apartments and the hotel via the public space, avoiding conflicts in use between the different programs. In this concept, each of the existing vertical cores would serve two different programs, which led us to identify dedicated elevators for each program, allowing for different users to travel independently inside the

existing elevator shafts. The zebra-like alternation of programs around the single-height floors of each core must be understood as a direct consequence of the central double-height Volume Capable scheme, combined with the ambition to reduce the number of office floors from 28 (in two distinct towers) to 14 large, connected, and continuous office floors. The stratification of programs, which naturally resulted from the other design strategies, was meticulously analyzed and evaluated during several months by both the design team and the owners. After these several months, it was decided that the various benefits of the zebra scheme outweighed the technical concerns it might raise. The zebra scheme is undoubtedly one of the best examples of how the design process managed to challenge fundamental certainties of the commercial real-estate market by introducing a smart and truly hand-tailored solution for a problem. Time will tell whether the zebra scheme can be adapted or applied to other projects and situations. For us as planners it demonstrates one of the most rewarding results of the intense collaborative design process, which brought together so many different disciplines and backgrounds in the project atelier. The atelier had created a prolific environment built on mutual trust between project partners, making it possible to push conventional boundaries in the interest of the project.

3. How to make a city

The large plinth of the World Trade Center had been planned and built as a shopping-mall-like urban interior, lacking relation to the public space and the neighborhood. For us, the future project had to find strategies to radically change the way the building engaged with the Northern Quarter and the city.

The program of the future project, combined with the spatial reorganization of the existing building, required creating three distinct access points to the cores (two on the ground floor and one on the first). This was an opportunity to reinvent the way the building addressed its surroundings and translated into three distinct urban addresses on three different streets surrounding the plot. Each program and access was organized in an attempt to recontextualize the building in its urban environment. Access to the hotel was positioned on Boulevard du Roi Albert II, roughly where the original access of the WTC had been (using the core of the former WTC I tower). The apartments were organized on Chaussée d'Anvers, facing Maximilian Park and the canal in the west. Access to the elevated lobby of the offices, spanning both cores, was organized along Boulevard Simon Bolívar, creating a strong new address as well as a physical link between the Northern Quarter and the development along the canal. At the southeast corner of the site, facing Gare du Nord, we positioned a roughly 2,000-square-meter greenhouse, which symbolizes most clearly the ambition of the project to reopen the site toward the city, participating in an effort to create a new, more mixed, resilient, and public form of urban habitat in the Northern Quarter.

Which Role for the Architect?

The interview took place on 9 July 2021 on the rooftop of WTC IV.

A Discussion with Johan Anrys and John Eyers

Moderated by Roxane Le Grelle

RLG Roxane Le Grelle
JE John Eyers
JA Johan Anrys

RLG   After a preparatory analysis of the site, you, John Eyers, took part in the jury of the second competition for the WTC towers launched in 2017 by Befimmo in collaboration with BMA Kristiaan Borret. Was it a requirement to create a temporary association between Jaspers-Eyers and the winner afterward? And did this affect the way you participated in the discussion as a member of the jury?

JE   We've been involved in this project from the word 'go' and have been working on it for years. That's why Befimmo had invited us to sit on the jury. As members of the jury, we looked at who best met the brief and submitted a project that could be used as an example for future building redevelopment projects. So the potential cooperation was not an issue during the judging. What's more, I didn't know Johan at the time.

For the first competition, Befimmo wanted to work with international firms such as OMA, UN Studio, or LAN. This culminated in an international architecture that is not grafted on the context. I'm rather oversimplifying things, but architecture is then an abstract element that can be positioned here in Brussels's Northern or Southern Quarter, or anywhere else for that matter.

The interesting thing about this project, when it was first proposed, was that there was a kind of mix between existing towers and a new building. That demonstrated a kind of connection with the surroundings, with Brussels. That's why the architecture of the other projects was not bad, but they lacked a sense of the context. This project was selected because it offers a solution to a social problem and anchors the city. It offers an opportunity! The needs of the Northern Quarter are addressed in this project. The rear of the building faces its surroundings by providing a different, lower volume. And the towers themselves, with their double-height levels, also provide a contextual solution. The two existing towers are linked so that the levels of the existing towers are compensated by the heights in the middle. These central spaces make it possible to preserve the existing building without it detracting from the overall project.

ZIN had the best starting point and integrated a number of elements that felt strong and weren't present in the other proposals. Integration into the environment was a very important focus for us. It was then jointly decided which project would best meet the future demands of the Flemish community, for example. Because we knew that this competition was about to take place. That was the deciding factor. It was as simple as that.

RLG So you were aware that the Flemish Government would be a possible end user of the building at the time of the competition?

JA It was there virtually, yes. The idea behind organizing the competition was for Befimmo to find a second architect who, together with Jaspers-Eyers, would prepare the project for the Flemish Government. As a team—51N4E, l'AUC, Jaspers-Eyers, and Befimmo—a proposal was then jointly drafted.

In the event of a long-term lease involving the Flemish Government, there would be a sufficient basic income to also develop the other conditions present in the project; the mix, the residential side, the greenhouse, and so on. All this comes at a cost, along with management costs for keeping the public space open, maintaining it and lighting it, for example. So this had a huge impact on the feasibility of the project.

RLG In other words, ZIN could never have gone ahead without the Flemish Government.

JA No, that's right, never.

JE And the advantage of this project for the Flemish Government is that it addresses a social question which is posed by the sanitary crisis. ZIN is, in fact, the first building that has adopted a new way of working. Today, we are one step further. That's why the quality of the project lies, among other things, in the large plateaus that allow for a different way of working in the future. Another important advantage is that the building can adapt itself in a flexible way to try to respond to any social issues that may crop up. In addition to integration with the environment, allowing a certain flexibility and offering a pleasant working atmosphere are also fundamental to the project.

We were lucky to work with an investor who saw the positive side of this and who has become an example for many. So in that respect, the project has had a key role in galvanizing everyone into action and making them think.

JA That's right. ZIN, through its mix, has created a certain standard and expectation that is actually a problem for the other buildings.

One of the things where ZIN really changes the mindset is the way the building is no longer a stand-alone building but organizes the public space and all the infrastructure in front of it. What ZIN really does, and it is consciously designed that way, is make the infrastructure downstairs available to third parties. The greenhouse is, of course, the most obvious example, but its extension is the auditorium. And it is precisely for these different reasons that this is an exceptional project. It's as if we were working in a vacuum.

RLG So as a real-estate investor, Befimmo plays a significant role in the development of this project. They endorse several experimental aspects, which is fundamental to achieving ZIN. What do you think is their USP?

JA Actually, it's a chance meeting of different parties. On the one hand, there's Befimmo, an investor and not a developer. I think this is crucial to the story because they project a long-term vision. They're committed to leasing the buildings, which is consistent with the circular philosophy. What was perhaps not sexy is now becoming sexy again in a way. They work with long-term funding and don't write off in 20 years. If you don't have this long-term vision, you can't really develop sustainable concepts. In addition, there's a very ambitious tenant who's setting the bar very high to become a pioneer in its role as a government and to set an example. As the third party, the designers are fundamentally important. In the team, we're also working on an urban planning level, so we don't just look at a building from a logical and programmatic point of view. The ambition is to develop new expertise, and that mainly lies in the way architecture—that building and that function—suddenly becomes part of the environment and creates a dynamic. The campus vibe. If the Northern Quarter is to be saved, it's going to be because it's set to become a campus.

JE So that's right, there has to be a click between a number of parties who together can make a project like ZIN possible and set an example for everyone. In this case, as you say, it's a chance meeting.

JA Befimmo's USP in this story is its long-term vision. And in the future, we want to work with investors for the sake of sustainability whenever we can.

RLG Besides the tenant and the investor, you mention the role of the designers in the realization of the project. This is indeed an important aspect that I would like to address. What role does the architect play in this process?

JA It's incredibly diverse. And I notice that this has also been what has been driving the complementarity between us, because we're enormously diverse in what we realize and, above all, connect. We're psychiatrist, philosopher, economist, contractor, technician, and a bit of everything else, all rolled into one.

JE I think so too! Our task is to think along with, and anticipate, the social evolution that is taking place. How can we be of service to society tomorrow and how can we offer an environment that is tailored to the world we all live in today?

JA In the ZIN project, as an architect you have to know where you want to make a change in quality, but you also have to know which preconditions you have to consider if you want the project to ever reach completion. As an architect, you keep so many plates spinning in the air, it's also just about trial and error. With the idea of the double-height spaces, the question was whether this would be feasible. How could we develop it as rationally as possible to keep the cost down? Because you have to assess things according to their feasibility and affordability. On the other hand, you also have to look for where the quality lies and whether that quality will actually add value to what we're looking for today. How is that quality translated? Is it in extra height or changeability?

JE Our task as architects is to constantly challenge the imagination. In addition, you have to dare to hold on to a few principles and go for them, because otherwise the project will become diluted. It's about the result, about what the best solution is. As an architect, that's the most important thing you have to deal with, the result you achieve. But it's a constant balancing act.

RLG In this kind of process, there's also an important alliance with the contractor. You have to ask whether it's a constructive relationship. What does it make possible or impossible?

JE I'm convinced that cooperation between the contractor, the architect, and the client is essential in order to achieve a sound solution. In a theoretical model, I would therefore say that this is indeed constructive. There are various ways to achieve a result, but it's always a trade-off. In my opinion, a contractor must play an important role in this.

JA I'm also convinced that a sound project is one that is driven by the contractor. Some contractors come up with their own suggestions, and I always tend to create that constructive vibe on a site and try to understand what makes a contractor able to do, or not do, certain things and why. I also expect the contractor to have a good understanding of the objectives related to a project so that, based on the preconditions he imposes, he can look for ways to overcome any obstacles and get the job done. Because then the objectives cannot be questioned.

We architects have to draw up tenders, but we can't know everything, that's impossible. In public tenders, architects are expected to know how the building is constructed, down to the last nail, but that's simply impossible. And the bigger the tender, the harder it is. And I'm also starting to see at ZIN that the price is not only driven by the technical dossier but also by a lot of market-related competition. That has a much bigger impact on price than we architects can quantify in our technical file.

JE It's like you say, you have to try to meet your goals, but starting from what exists on the market in terms of expertise. And existing elements may need to be adapted, but it's not appropriate in large projects to draw things to size if they exist on the market. You may be able to do so in a smaller project, but large projects don't allow for that.

JA No, for projects the size of ZIN, architects can't take all of the responsibility. You tend to put together existing projects. Nevertheless, it's how they come together that matters.

It takes a lot of energy and it's hard to enter into dialogue with the contractor and to make clear what we're looking for and how things should be done. Actually, that's a kind of battle, a constant bargaining where we're always looking to keep the margins as wide as possible.

It's a constructive battle, because you have to constantly challenge contractors. As an architect, in the ideal scenario, you also need to be a kind of person who is able to establish a sense of cohesion for such a building and draw up common objectives and say, in terms of content, what we're looking for. And every time there are problems, to refer to them and see how can we overcome them and where can we find a support base and a compromise of what we do, it's a give-and-take.

In the ZIN project, as an architect you have to know where you want to make a change in quality, but you also have to know which pre-conditions you have to consider if you want the project to ever reach completion.

RLG Roxane Le Grelle
JE   John Eyers
JA   Johan Anrys

JE Those interests between architects and contractors are different. And there are so many interests. Because in addition to the investor, the architect, and the contractor, you also have the end user. And for ZIN, the process is even more complicated because the end user, the Flemish Government, has set the bar very high. Material passports, TOTEM (total energy module), GRO—these are all things you don't have with other customers.[1]

JA The only thing we can do as architects is to bring all those ambitions together into an acceptable whole. All I can do is propose some kind of architectural solution that I think will strike the right balance between all of them. Actually, as an architect you are a bit of a mediator where you also play a little with those interests. For example, we use the sustainability meter and the standards imposed by the Flemish Government to challenge Befimmo.

JE And the Flemish Government uses us to ensure that the contractor delivers what they expect for the GRO. So as an architect, you're a bit of a middleman. It's almost like a politician who has to form a government at some point. And you don't have the luxury of ten competent people to bring all those different political parties together and say, at the end of the day, we have an agreement. That's actually what an architect does. It's bringing different parties to the table. You have to strike a compromise between interests that are all different.

JA In that sense, it is actually a question of politics. And you have to be able to live with not 'the best project' but 'the best possible project.'

JE That's very well said. Indeed, you will never achieve 100 per cent of what you want.

JA The question is, is 'the good enough project' good enough? I always try to clarify that for myself. When I'm standing in front of that building, I never want to get to the situation where I say, I could have done a better job. I'm not going to do that, because if I do, you stab someone in the back. You have to say, 'That's the best I could do under those circumstances, and I did everything I could and I can't do any better than that.' You have to be able to say that. Then you can face everyone with your head held high. And that has to be the starting point. And with that starting point, everyone has to be on board. That's how you build trust.

JE That's the idea. That's a goal. And the idea is to achieve it as well as possible. Architects can't solve everything on their own; it's a team effort, and we have to make sure we're all singing from the same hymn sheet and make sure we achieve the goals using what's available on the market in terms of expertise. Then, as you say, you achieve 'the best possible project.'

1. Gro is a Nordic woman's name and means 'growth.' This term is used as a sustainability measure in Flanders.

Amar Lalvani
and Bernard Dubois

This interview took place via video chat on 24 March 2021.

Interview
by Alessandro Gess

AG   Alessandro Gess
AL   Amar Lalvani
BD   Bernard Dubois

AG   Amar, I recently read an interview in which you describe how, as a result of travel restrictions, your hotels were increasingly occupied by locals, people looking for a break and a vacation in their hometown. I find this a really interesting phenomenon, because it shows that hotels can be meaningful local actors in a community. All the Standard Hotels I have visited so far combine an international, metropolitan dimension with a strong anchorage in the local community. Will the Standard Brussels become such a place of interest for both international visitors and the local community?

AL   For sure. Interestingly, even before the crisis, a majority of the people who came to our restaurants, bars, and nightclubs were local already. Of course, the hotel rooms were mostly visitors, even though, because of travel restrictions last year, our hotel guests were increasingly locals. After being stuck at home for weeks, people were looking for a different moment and experience in their own city. Our hotels are always a local hub, and now people are using hotels differently, obviously. I think this is relevant as well for Brussels. When I came here to visit the site in the Northern Quarter, I could feel a new dynamic in the city. I lived here about 15 years ago, so I know Brussels quite well. I was surprised to rediscover the city and to feel how things have changed. The dynamic art and design scene and the urban development happening on the canal with Kanal-Pompidou coming represent a great potential for the city. I'm convinced that Brussels will become more attractive for European and international visitors but also for the many people living outside the city in the region. Those people will come to Brussels to experience their own city in a different way and even stay over on the weekends. I think this is going to be fascinating. As I said from the beginning, I would love for people in Paris and London who are dismissive of Brussels to actually leave their cities and come to Brussels for the weekend and think, Oh my god, this is an undiscovered gem. What the pandemic has also shown is that people are realizing there are many places close to home that are very interesting. You don't have to go far away to find places that are interesting. I think Brussels can be that type of destination.

BD   That idea of a destination close to home is interesting because indeed we are really discovering the city more and in a different way. The center of Brussels has greatly evolved in recent years. It is not only about gentrification. As in many cities, the historical center has increasingly lost its inhabitants and has been strongly marked by tourism. As a result, in recent years, different new urban centers have emerged where the local community is really alive. This is the case, for example, behind Place Sainte-Catherine, close to the canal, and you can feel how this dynamic is progressively moving toward the Northern Quarter.

AG   Do you see parallels between the situation of the Standard Hotel in the Northern Quarter with other Standard Hotels? I'm thinking of downtown LA, which is situated in a mono-programmatic business district, or Kings Cross, which is right across the street from one of London's busiest train stations.

AL   When we did downtown LA, there was nothing like what we did, but we had some belief that our concept was going to be a success. It was a big market, with people coming to downtown LA every day to work, but with nothing fun to do. It's a very simple concept. Everybody wants to have some fun. So that was an easy idea. The Meatpacking District was another one. You could see Chelsea, the galleries, the West Village becoming a very good place to live. You could see the benefits of being on the water, you could trust something was going to be interesting about the High Line park, you could see these dynamics coming together. But to take the plunge and say, We're going to go ahead and do that, takes some forethought but also some belief that you can create something special that had to be something significant. Kings Cross in London is another one. When we started looking at that project, many people thought the building was ugly, they didn't like the brutalism. No one even noticed the building because it was a gray government office building. We looked at it and said, Wow, this looks like the building we wanted the Standard High Line to look like. It actually existed already under everybody's nose, and in fact what I love about that building is that every other group that looked at it wanted to tear it down, and we were the only ones that wanted to preserve it, and we enhanced it and cleaned it up and preserved the windows and did everything. And when I talked about that seven or eight years ago when we started the project, everybody said, Kings Cross is a trashy area, it's a red-light district, it's for commuters and it's not interesting. But the Eurostar was coming in right across the street, and we could see that Google was putting in their headquarters, and it is actually the geographic center of London, even if no one ever thinks about it that way. It is not east, south, north, or west. We saw things in it that others dismissed. I think this project here in Brussels has very similar attributes, both looking at the urban potential surrounding it and its situation in the city. When I first came to see the WTC towers and the site in 2019, I was excited to see that, in contrast to 15 years ago, there were young people living in the city, there was movement, there was action.
        For the Standard, we look at how places change and we're excited to be ahead of the curve and anchor our places with something that is cultural. When I lived here I was working in the Northern Quarter. Our head offices were at the Sheraton, which is very close to the project site. In the Northern Quarter you can experience the result of the 'Brusselization' of the 1970s, with its desire to attract these global corporate headquarters. And you can see some of the errors that were made, which led to a form of resistance from the local community. Some of the errors were made frankly without planning, without thought, without thinking about the culture, and so on. You got these monolithic office buildings put in the center of the city that not surprisingly never developed life around them and were dismissed as negative and probably caused some of the negative feelings toward Brussels. This project, with the Standard being involved, with you doing such innovative and effective architecture, opening up to the city, bringing in greenery, inviting the city in as opposed to leaving the city out—I won't say it is an opportunity to rectify those mistakes, but it is an opportunity to do perhaps what should have been done and turn it into what it always should have been but never became.

Five learning points for the future from the involvement of the editors in the Brussels Northern Quarter from 2017 to today, meant to inspire the debate on the planning of and realization of projects. Each point refers to one or more of the texts included or documents mentioned in this publication.

1.

FOSTER AN ECOSYSTEM OF DIVERSITY

Can the Northern Quarter turn diversity into an asset, with places for large and small organizations, and with different levels of rent, ranging from high end to rough and ready?

2.

SHARE THE AVAILABLE SPACE

Can meeting rooms, workshop spaces, board rooms, and sports facilities be shared by a diversity of users beyond the nine-to-five, during the week, and on the weekend?

3.

EMBRACE THE ENERGY TRANSITION

Can a shift in the energy supply, powered by the bigger users in the quarter, create a district that is fully free of fossil fuels?

4.

NURTURE A MULTIPLE HABITAT

Can the excess of open space become a habitat, a haven of biodiversity for the neighborhood and beyond, a huge stepping stone in a larger blue-green network?

5.

DIVERSIFY FORMS OF LIVING

Can the large building stock be rethought and reused for other more generous and more collective forms of living, on scales and with sizes not possible in the more traditional urban fabric?

Werner Joris, former Chief of Business Development at Befimmo

Excerpts of an interview that took place on 17 January 2019 at BOZAR Café Victor in Brussels.

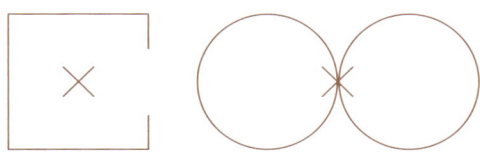

Interview by Alessandro Gess

AG   Alessandro Gess
WJ   Werner Joris

AG   Unlike many other buildings in the Northern Quarter, the World Trade Center was a multi-tenant structure and a joint ownership. As such, could you describe how the project started for you and explain the steps which led to the decision to transform WTC I and II?

WJ   Befimmo was leasing large parts of the plinth and the entire tower of WTC II to the public administration (Belgian Buildings Agency). Their lease was coming to an end in late 2018, so it was urgent for us to plan for the future. Three years prior to their departure, we began to think about what we could do with the building. The fact that we only controlled about half of the complex didn't make things easier for us. Since co-ownership compromised the development possibilities of the complex, we decided to try and acquire the other parts of the building. These were owned by many different institutional and private owners. We hoped this would simplify the transformation of WTC I and II. This process took several years. In parallel to the acquisition strategy, we organized the first competition to imagine the future architectural project. But much to our disappointment, the competition failed to produce a convincing design.

AG   Can you explain the first competition procedure and why, in your eyes, it failed? Viewing the proposals, I was surprised to see that most architects intended to raze the complex. Was demolition of the WTC something you imposed?

WJ   No, the architects decided that independently. Back then, only the project by LAN proposed to keep the existing WTC. They added a new exterior steel structure which allowed to add floors to the existing project. They had analyzed the typical plan of the WTC, which according to them was extremely efficient and justified the preservation. They carried out a comparative analysis with other office buildings to demonstrate the great quality of the floor layout of the existing towers. All architects proposed important changes to the plinth. It was universally identified as the major point creating dysfunction between the public space and the ground floor. But somehow all the projects in the competition lacked specificity: they could have been anywhere. We weren't satisfied with the result and it was impossible to select a winning entry. After this, Jaspers-Eyers, who had been involved in the Northern Quarter on our behalf, continued with a programmatic feasibility study.

AG   I assume that by involving the Brussels-Capital Region in the second competition you were hoping to arrive at a more specific response? How did the region, how did Kristiaan Borret (government architect), influence the way you organized the second tender?

WJ   Initially the region was very focused on the Canal Plan. They hadn't really been involved in the transformation of the Northern Quarter. The WTC was in that sense a first collaborative experiment between the real-estate world and the region. Kristiaan Borret imposed the idea of an open call, meaning that we couldn't draw up our own short list of architects. This was new to us and meant that we were suddenly confronted with architects we didn't know. From the many applications we received, we collectively short-listed some architects with the region. That's how we got to know you! The organization of the open call was one of the main conditions of the region for being part of the process. The public authorities also demanded that the redevelopment include housing so as to break up the monofunctionality of the Northern Quarter.

AG I understand from our previous conversations that involving the region in such an early phase of the project was very new for the company and that it was a controversial decision?

WJ Yes. After the first competition, there were discussions at Befimmo about the future strategy to adopt. My position internally was that we could not, on the one hand, promote change in the Northern Quarter with the Up4North initiatives and, on the other hand, propose the classic real-estate procedure to the region in which we would develop a project internally without involving them. I was able to convince the CEO of Befimmo to accept an open competition organized via the Bouwmeester, or Brussels government architect. It was not easy, since there is a level of distrust between the private real-estate sector and the new type of project governance the Bouwmeester stands for. I had met him during my years in real-estate development in Antwerp, where he was city architect at the time. We knew each other and had mutual trust. After I was appointed chief of business development for Befimmo, we met during an event in the Northern Quarter, and that's when we started to discuss the possible involvement of the region in the competition.

AG At this point, the transitory occupation of WTC I was already ongoing. Do you think this redefined your position toward the existing building? I'm asking this because for us, as planners, it definitely did. To work on-site in the project atelier on the 15th floor was fantastic. It allowed us to really understand the building as well as the Northern Quarter as a whole. During these months, the building became a test site that allowed for experimentation. I'm convinced that we wouldn't have designed the project the same way if we hadn't been on-site.

WJ The transitory occupation and the collective work on the design in the atelier clearly helped to change the attachment people at Befimmo had for the building. It really made it possible to approach this project differently. I think that today at Befimmo we would even reconsider a simple renovation of the towers if the Flemish Government were going to choose another site.

AG Were you aware at this point that the Flemish Government was looking for a large office building and was going to launch a tender procedure? Also, the notion of circularity has played a very important role in the tender process. How did it influence decision-making on your site?

WJ We knew that the Flemish Government was planning to reorganize but we didn't know when, and we had no information about the size of the building and so forth. We simply had to envision a future for the building since our last tenant was going to leave it by the end of 2018. The WTC is a very important part of our portfolio, so it was urgent to plan for the future. It was pure coincidence that the tender of the Flemish Government was published around the same time and that everything fit in perfectly with our planning. It is true that the tender procedure of the Flemish Government influenced a lot of things. The environmental standards of the Flemish Government

The WTC was in that sense a first collaborative experiment between the real-estate world and the region. Kristiaan Borret imposed the idea of an open call, meaning that we couldn't draw up our own short list of architects. This was new to us and meant that we were suddenly confronted with architects we didn't know.

At Befimmo we initially believed that the new project would be a cosmetic rehabilitation of the two existing towers. This changed when you submitted your design.

forced us, forced everyone to think differently. Look at the material passport, for example, which is quite extraordinary. We never had done anything like this.

AG   I agree. By analyzing the composition of the existing building, you rediscover the capacity of the built substance to be transformed, recycled, or upgraded. Do you feel that there has been a shift toward more circular design approaches in the industry?

WJ   The policy of the Flemish Government is unique. It drove the process. Unfortunately, I don't feel that ambition elsewhere, neither in other administrations like here in Brussels nor in the private sector. I hope this will change.

AG   How did you perceive our first design proposal during the competition procedure?

WJ   At Befimmo we initially believed that the new project would be a cosmetic rehabilitation of the two existing towers. This changed when you submitted your design. The model in particular had a big impact. It changed everything—even for John [Eyers], who was part of the jury. I remember standing next to him during the presentation. He looked at all the plans, then turned to me and said, 'I'm impressed, this is brilliant.'

AG   The project challenges many of the typical norms of commercial real estate. We were surprised to discover that it wasn't too difficult to challenge those norms and that there was a lot of room for discussion. How was the project perceived in the city's real-estate market, considering the unconventional proportion of spaces and the programmatic mix?

WJ   The project was in many regards exploratory. Concerning the spaces, the heavy transformation, and the mixed use, we had no comparison and no experience. That's why we saw potential project partners during the design phase so as to confront them with the design. We were all quite surprised by the very positive feedback. Very few concerns were raised. This helped to reassure both ourselves and the stakeholders. The project helped to challenge the way we work internally. I believe that our project will have an impact in the Brussels real-estate world. Developers copy each other. It's a very traditional world, where things are rarely questioned. That's why developers drag concepts from one project to another.

AG   Brussels has a very particular relation with commercial real estate, which marked the city's development after the World's Fair and later with the arrival of the European institutions. The WTC and the Northern Quarter as a whole are symbolic of the devastating side effects of commercial real estate in the city. How does the presence of large institutions like the European Union influence the way developers build?

WJ   The EU is partly responsible for the monotony of office typologies in the city. Their standards are very strict and have become a sort of universal guideline here in Brussels, since all developers want to potentially rent space to the EU. Unfortunately, the standards are neither very good nor innovative, on the contrary. From an investor's viewpoint, what I can say is that we are aware of the need for change. We as investors are here for the long term, which means that we have a genuine interest in investing in the quality of our real-estate portfolio. The role of actors such as Kristiaan Borret is very important also to help move the lines and norms. It is possible to challenge collectively the way we build. That's what convinced us during the work on the WTC. You shouldn't take anything for granted and you should question the way things are.

Almut Fuhr of the Flemish Government, interview in *Circubuild*, October 2, 2020, https://www.circubuild.be/nl/nieuws/almut-fuhr-het-facilitair -bedrijf-over-kantoor-2023-gunningscriteria-in-aanbestedingen-zullen-meer-en-meer-richting-circulair-bouwen-evolueren/.

'The size of the project (110,000 m² in total) naturally makes it easier to get a design team—as well as contractors and manufacturers—to comply with circular criteria. In the future, circular award criteria will become the standard in tendering procedures. We are working on that, but the transition to new construction methods naturally takes time, including as regards contractors and suppliers. This does not mean that we are not paying attention to circular construction in our building proce-dures today. Here, too, we try to encourage design teams to think about how their design can be made more circular. We give them tools to do so, including the GRO. But in such a classical procedure, there is no link between the design team and the contractor, and the price often remains the decisive factor. The choice of whether or not to take the circular route is primarily an ideological one.'

Almut Fuhr

Roeland Dudal

The Glass Trojan Horse*

* This text is an elaboration of an earlier version published in *A+ 278 Brussels*, June 2019.

According to the traditional media sources, there seems to be a consensus about the future of the Northern Quarter. The outdated, monofunctional office district, which remains empty and gray after office hours, will in the future be mixed, multiple, resilient, urban, and innovative. This shouldn't prove hard given its excellent location in the Brussels metropolis, situated as it is between the busiest train station and the future museum of contemporary art in the iconic Citroën garage—and where, to boot, the strongest players in the Brussels real-estate world have the bulk of the land ownership sitting in their portfolios.

It is a district with a precarious and painful history. With great fanfare, it was heralded as the Manhattan of Europe. The Northern Quarter was created as part of a flat clean-up policy. It was completed at a time when speculation in the city was the dominant logic, meaning that the balance between public and private interests was not achieved as proclaimed. Vast amounts of precious raw materials were sunk into a neighborhood that, just thirty to forty years later, is once again poised for a thorough transformation. It is an ailing district.

Many point to the momentum generated by linking the ongoing conversion of this district to the social transitions and needs that feature on the agenda with ever-increasing prominence. The Northern Quarter as a laboratory for the future of the city. *The Future Is Here*. But what does this really mean? Whose future is it? What added values are created and who is riding the wave of success? More and more people are concerned about the answers to these questions after calculating the results of the first rush of attention.

The year 2018 was brimming with initiatives that saw renewed potential in the Northern Quarter, all of which aimed to contribute, in their own way, to a vision for the future of the district. The Faculty of Architecture of KU Leuven set up a temporary school space, Samenlevingsopbouw began testing new housing forms in old offices, Marcel Bike Café installed a temporary social bicycle repair area, an urban roof garden arose between the glass towers … Each of the above initiatives aims to examine how things can be done differently and better. They're valuable and fragile at the same time.

After all, they share a common agenda that is not very clear, and there is no public mandate. The creation of this agenda is not shared publicly. Research projects overlap and precious time is lost.

Precious time, since the Northern Quarter is already in the throes of transformation: buildings are being demolished, rebuilt, or renovated. With 'Zin in Noord,' the future project for the WTC I and II towers, the transition to a new real-estate trend may prove final. But it takes time to change urban-development practices. The consequences of today's real-estate decisions will only become visible further down the line and policy innovation is slow, while social emergencies and socio-spatial issues are accumulating ever more rapidly. Making the right connections between public needs and private dynamics is difficult because of the different speeds involved.

As a think-and-do-tank, Architecture Workroom Brussels has stepped into the dynamics of temporary use and the call for the creation of a collective vision for the Northern Quarter. If we, as an architecture organization, not only want to contribute to the discussion about 'being right,' but if we also want to have an impact on the practice of 'being right,' then we need to get our hands dirty from time to time. Like many other small creative businesses, we moved into a temporary office in the WTC I tower in the Northern Quarter in Brussels. As curators, we also organized the cultural event *You Are Here*, a program of exhibitions, urban debates, and a shared workspace, in the framework of the International Architecture Biennale of Rotterdam. To achieve this, we teamed up with various associations, administrations, and entrepreneurs. As the culmination of the 'parcours' through the building from the street to the 23rd floor, the World Trade Center was occasionally renamed the World Transformation Center. A shared workspace hosted more than 400 actors and 150 events to exchange knowledge on the major societal transitions within a shared agenda for a more qualitative and sustainable societal and spatial transformation of our cities and landscape.

The Faculty of Architecture of KU Leuven was also present. The 24th floor was their campus outside the campus. The school outside the school. Why did an architecture school want to contribute to the above dynamics in the Northern Quarter? Similar considerations as above were raised. Students were confronted with their position inside or outside the school, inside or outside the real world. Are we in or above the city?

The yearly Springweek workshop took place in WTC I and addressed this question. The Springweek is an intensive four-day exercise. During that time, all bachelor's students take on an exceptional task together. From morning to night they work in teams on a collective project. What is the position of the architect on the 24th floor of a former office tower, thinking about his contribution to the city, with a beautiful view on the subject of his study? Where should the architect be: in the school, in his ivory tower, or in the city? The fact that Wim Cuyvers, as guest lecturer, prohibited students from taking such a position was very refreshing. They examined the immediate edges of

Critical proximity. This describes the experiences of many of the temporary users who occupied WTC I for eighteen months. But is this really possible? Can you be critical of the surroundings in which you are embedded? Can you distance yourself from the comfort of the creative ecosystem of which you are a part?

the WTC complex and its problematic dialogue with the surrounding public space and its users: local residents, the homeless, people on the run. Up-close confrontation.

Critical proximity. This describes the experiences of many of the temporary users who occupied WTC I for eighteen months. But is this really possible? Can you be critical of the surroundings in which you are embedded? Can you distance yourself from the comfort of the creative ecosystem of which you are a part? For example, with the exception of 51N4E, none of the users of WTC I had any say in the plans that were drawn up for the premises. The future of the building was determined by means of a procedure. The procedure led to secrecy. It was impossible to instigate an open and transparent process of co-design for the building. How could we fool ourselves into working on the future of the city without a mandate to actually shape that future?

While the shoe of principle might have pinched, the coat of pragmatism fit like a glove. The generosity of the building owner, Befimmo—who made thousands of square meters of space available almost free of charge at a prime location with a phenomenal view of the city, who indirectly placed their best minds at our disposal, and for whom no practical question was too much—is praiseworthy. Of course, this also served their own agenda. That was not a secret. It was clear from the outset.

Were we naive when we enthusiastically saw *The Future Is Here* appear on the facade of WTC I? Naturally, the dynamics of such initiatives increase the development potential and consequently the market demand for the activated sites. Yes, it is problematic if only trendy, creative, and artistic practices are given access to the precarious use projects while real needs—such as the humane reception of refugees, affordable housing for vulnerable groups, and space for socioeconomic initiatives, for example—find no place within the temporary city. This is the most pressing question of all: for whom, and for whose benefit, are we making these efforts?

Real-estate logic that only relies on temporary use as a cover for problematic vacancy management and advocates the traditional profit models is unacceptable. We must up the stakes and raise the bar. But this bar must be set by the public authorities who serve the general interest, not by the private parties (alone). In order to realize these ambitions, new collaborations and alternative practices need to emerge that transcend the traditional dichotomy between private and public interests. To this end, temporary use as an in-between space offers a unique opportunity to arrive at new agreements, value frameworks, and real-estate models through unexpected encounters and experimental alliances.

City movements such as BRAL and Inter-Environnement Bruxelles detect in the WTC I temporary use project, and by extension in many other schemes in Brussels, merely a diversionary tactic that disguises the urgent need for change with a hint of good intentions. But we can also read the application of temporary use as a glass Trojan Horse. An offer for a social revolution and a spatial transformation from the inside out. Not hostile and closed, but open and transparent.

The horse may have been put in the stable for a while, but it's still there. Who is willing to join this adventure, to argue from within—in complete transparency—as the foot soldiers of everyone's interests, and to change the model of city-making? Who's going to give the people in power a thorough shake-up?

Mathieu Berger and Louise Carlier, 'Introduction,' in *Whose Future Is Here? Searching for Hospitality in the Brussels North Quarter,*
ARCH (Action Research Collective for Hospitality), 2019, p. 3.

'While the attention of many urban actors is now focused on the Northern Quarter, there is little consideration of the problems addressed by the occupation of the neighbourhood by migrants—as evidenced by the diagnoses and programmes underway in this territory. The humanitarian situation there was marginalized in the spaces for reflection and debate on its development; the perspective of the actors of hospitality and hospitality is itself absent. The presence of migrants tends to be considered as an episode with which it is not necessary to deal in this area of public action. However, the Northern Quarter, as a station district, is historically a neighbourhood of arrival and first settlement for newcomers in precarious situations in Brussels, from which their gradual inclusion in different areas of social and urban life is determined.'

Mathieu Berger
& Louise Carlier

Jan Denoo

On Scientists and Lab Rats in the Experimental City

INTRODUCTION

Modernism killed the past. Postmodernism killed the future. Today, a new planning paradigm is emerging in this 'temporal rupture from both sides' (Madanipour, 2010: 355). Rejecting lessons from the past and visions for the future, 'urban experimentation' is being proposed in public and private spheres as a new narrative that enables thinking about and acting upon the city between a contested present and an uncertain future (Abbott, 2005; Caprotti & Cowley, 2017; Davies, 2010; Evans, 2016; Hodson, Evans & Schliwa, 2018; Karvonen & van Heur, 2014; Powell & Vasudevan, 2007). Exchanging secluded test sites for complex society (Gross & Krohn, 2005; Heathcott, 2005) and clear hypotheses for open-endedness (Evans, 2016; Karvonen & van Heur, 2014; Kenny & Meadowcroft, 1999; Meadowcroft, 2009), 'urban experimentation' is being resurrected from its pragmatist past as a new way to deal with the *raison d'être* of planning: uncertainty (Dewey, 1929; Park, 1929; Caprotti & Cowley, 2017; J. Evans, 2016; Andrew Karvonen & van Heur, 2014).

Merging with this laboratorization of the urban is the rising practice of temporary use (Madanipour, 2018). Next to (i) 'preventing decay' and (ii) 'revitalising its surrounding context,' this practice is often framed as a 'lab' in which to (iii) test out structures and programs on a scale that is bound in temporal, spatial, and budgetary terms and that could inspire future projects (Evans, 2016). While the first two motivations for temporary use are often criticized as a tool for pumping up rent gaps and stirring up gentrification (Colomb, 2012; Ferreri, 2015; Harris, 2015; Madanipour, 2018; Tonkiss, 2013), this third argument is often staged to legitimize temporary use as constitutive of radical experiments that 'can open up cities to more radical agendas of change' (Karvonen, Evans & van Heur, 2014: 3).

In Brussels, a similar narrative is emerging. As stated by the Brussels government architect, or Bouwmeester, of the Brussels-Capital Region Kristiaan Borret, the 6,500,000 m² of vacant space in the region (Toestand, 2018) presents an opportunity for temporary use, as 'there is no deterioration awaiting the start of the construction project [and] there will be a fresh impulse for the neighborhood, or even a test phase, to uncover new ideas for the final project' (Bruzz, 2018).

After several small to medium-sized urban experiments in the capital, a new and large-scale one was introduced in its contested Northern Quarter —of which the World Trade Center (WTC) was part. The area in the north of the city can roughly be delineated by the small ring road, the canal, and the railroad. To understand and critically evaluate the current experimental framing of the development of the neighborhood, and the position of the WTC therein, it cannot be isolated from its paradigmatic, extreme, and contested planning history (Flyvberg, 2006). In the next part, the planning history of the Northern Quarter is revisited through the lens of 'uncertainty' to embed urban experimentation and the position of WTC24 in a brief history of planning as 'controlling uncertainty' (Marris, 1987: 159).

To embed this approach, one cannot ignore John Dewey's work on this topic. In *The Quest for Certainty*, he describes bridging the uncertainty between the known and the unknown as humankind's longest quest (Dewey, [1933] 1929). Besides animating everyday life, it constitutes the *raison d'être* of what has been professionalized in a plethora of planning practices. Alongside economic, environmental, and social planning, its urban variant seems to bundle the three as cities cluster global challenges and opportunities through the process of planetary urbanization (UN-Habitat, 2016; Benner, 2017). Although situated at the very heart of its practice, the perspective of uncertainty in analyzing urban planning is nearly uncharted (Abbott, 2005, 2009, 2012; Friend & Jessop, 1969; Healey, 2009; Hillier, 2013; Karvonen & van Heur, 2014a; Marris, 1987; Simone, 2013; Thrift, 2004).

TRANSCENDING UNCERTAINTY

After years of mourning and gradual reconstruction of the traumatic recent past, a new perspective on the future was developed in the post-WWII era. This perspective was reflected in modern urban planning that was already breeding earlier that century in the US, envisioning large-scale and ambitious new futures. The first radical but hesitant proposals for the Northern Quarter in 1928 by Victor Bourgeois, followed by those of Groupe Structures in the 1960s (Wonen TA/BK, 1975), led to a first wave of inhabitants leaving their homes, breaking away from the uncertainty hovering over the neighborhood. The fabricated decay that followed in certain streets was framed and generalized for the whole neighborhood as an 'urban disease' that, as in other parts of the world (Osborn, 1942; Beauregard, 1989; Gans, 1969; Harvey, 1989), was central to legitimizing an even larger plan for the neighborhood.

'My fellow citizens, Belgium is about to enter a new dimension. And the inhabitants of this country will be able to live wealthier lives and think more broadly. At least, if they are willing to do so.' Half a century ago, this government announcement was intended to prepare the Belgian population for one of the most ambitious urban development programs on the continent. Driven by a determined modernist optimism, building on the spirit of the World's Fair in 1958, the prime minister of Belgium Paul Vanden Boeynants presented the 'Manhattan Plan,' his latest collaboration with real-estate giant Charles 'Charly' De Pauw. With 'great urgency' and for 'the common good,' a radical tabula rasa development of the Brussels Northern Quarter was justified in the *Belgian Official Journal* of 1967. No fewer than 53,000 m² with 11,000 inhabitants or more than 3,000 families were expropriated and their houses destroyed (Martens, 2009) to build 'the navel of Europe' (Wonen TA / BK, 1975). The plan consisted of 58 office towers with a height of between 40 and 160 meters, all built on 13-meter plinths that would be connected by bridges to serve as an artificial pedestrian level as two highways —one connecting Amsterdam to the Mediterranean, the other connecting Istanbul with the Atlantic to London and the US—would cross on the ground level (Martens & Purnôde, 2011).

Transcending uncertainty between now and then, the manufactured malaise of the urban was framed as submissive to the curing power of the man-made future. The Manhattan Plan for the Northern Quarter approached the urban as both an anomaly and the symbol of modern life, captured in Le Corbusier's radio speech in which he describes his arrival by boat at the place where the plan's name got its inspiration:

> I saw rising in the morning mists a city which was fantastic and almost mystical. There is the temple of the new world, I thought. But as the boat drew nearer to the city the apparition in the mist was transformed into an image of brutality and savagery. This indeed is certainly the most obvious manifestation of modern times. This brutality and savagery do not necessarily displease me. For it is thus that all great work must begin—with strength. That evening on the avenues of the city I came to appreciate the American people who have been able, following some law of life which is their own, to create a race—a race of splendid men and beautiful women.

Le Corbusier, 1935

As sharply described in Giddens's *Runaway World* (1999), the optimism and risk calculations that were core to underpinning modernism, the major urban developments and the promises they held, could only be summarized as 'things haven't turned out that way' (p. 44). The controlled implosion of the modernist Pruitt-Igoe blocks in St. Louis, Missouri, in 1972 symbolized a turning point in the history of urban planning. In Brussels, the econometric risk calculation culture that blew over from France—a mode of thinking embedded in institutes like the Société Belge d'Économie et de Mathématiques Appliquées (SOBEMAP), which backed the socioeconomic 'common good' that the Manhattan Plan of Groupe Structures promised—also suffered a major hit. The risk calculation that was supposed to be 'a way of regulating the future, of normalizing it and bringing it under our dominion' (Giddens, 1999: 44) and the assumptions it made were abruptly confronted with the 1973 oil crisis. Its aftermath scarred the city. The €534 million of tax money invested in the project with a belief in its *trickle-down* effect only resulted in 22 per cent of the planned buildings, 43 per cent of the foreseen inhabitants, and around 30 per cent of the promised job positions in 2011 (Martens & Purnôde, 2011). Although this recent history only lives on in a few of its inhabitants, its heritage still echoes strongly in the present. Not only is its financial crater still being paid off by the inhabitants of the three municipalities that were involved, namely Brussels City, Sint-Joost-Ten-Node, and Schaerbeek, it is also still carved in its urban landscape as every visitor of Brussels's administrative center outside of the Northern Quarter—as well as those of a dozen of other buildings—still have to take a staircase to the first floor before taking the elevator, as they were all built on a plinth to connect with the elevated pedestrian level of the Northern Quarter.

REFRAMING UNCERTAINTY

The Manhattan Plan, together with other brutal developments such as the construction of the *jonction,* or North-South railway connection, and the European Quarter, is often labeled as *bruxellisation.* This notorious term is often defined as 'the capitalist destruction of the city with a compromising role of the public sector' (Lagrou, 2003) or 'a juxtaposition of buildings of different styles and the destruction of the pre-existing urban fabric' (Dumont, 2005). The trauma it imposed on the city and the 'villains' it created, as Isabelle Doucet (2012) puts it, were the basis of a new mode of thinking and planning the future. These events severely disrupted the stability that was essential to secure the stretched turnover time of the Fordist economies and its linear causality assumptions that propelled this mode of urban planning. As a result, as the temporal stability essential to Fordism evaporated, the shortening of temporal frames of investment served as an answer to the uncertainties in the various economic sectors (Harvey, 1989). If uncertainty generally exists in between the actual and the possible, and economically exists in between supply and an incalculable and fluctuating demand (Savini, 2017), a new *just-in-time* model of investment, production, and supply aims to narrow this gap (Monden, 2011; Harvey, 1989). Hence, uncertainty is reduced to a minimum so that it can be embedded in and embraced by this new economic system.

In Brussels, this new economic thinking was reflected in urban-planning practices that strongly limited its temporal and spatial boundaries and introduced participatory practices while easing its *blueprint-averse population.* More than anything, this new mode of urban planning is embodied in the Neighbourhood Contracts that started four

How to Produce Change?

years after the creation of the Brussels-Capital Region in 1989 and developed into the Sustainable Neighbourhood Contracts in 2010. The four-to-six-year redevelopments of limited perimeters with budgets of around €30 million were developed to patch up the socio-spatial ruptures in the city that are strongly connected to *bruxellisation*. By limiting the temporal, spatial, and budgetary boundaries, as well as by structurally embedding participation in the process, a more modest approach to planning the future was established.

TEST-TUBING UNCERTAINTY

Today, half a century after the introduction of the Manhattan Plan, new urban-planning narratives are emerging. As the threats of the patchworked urban landscape of Brussels are loosening, two reactions can be distinguished. On the one hand, building on the increased maturity of the region that is celebrating its thirtieth anniversary this year, as well as reacting to the growing chorus of voices calling for the regionalization of municipal responsibilities, various actions have been undertaken to address challenges that transcend local budgets and interests. The 2018 Regional Sustainable Development Plan, which looks toward both the 2025 and 2040 horizons, is the most telling example of this spatial and temporal upscaling. On the other hand, the rigidity of the Sustainable Neighbourhood Contracts to locally implement urban change has generated a new field of practice in which new modes of planning the city are trialed.

In the Northern Quarter, after 50 years of lagging development, both new dynamics are played out. On the one hand, as the canal is seen as the backbone of the Brussels Regional Sustainable Development Plan, the neighborhood's location along it drags it more directly into the spotlight. On the other hand, ironically, the people-centered approach as well as selection procedure of the Sustainable Neighbourhood Contracts meant that the expropriated and still scarcely inhabited part of the Northern Quarter, while being one of the most iconic cases of the 'bulldozer urbanism' it wanted to be an alternative to, was never subject to a new public rethinking and redevelopment program. This lack of public engagement on the local level was bound to confront the need for a new mode of planning this area.

Today, this turning point seems to have been reached. The biggest private owners of the office towers in the area, including Allianz Benelux, the biggest real-estate developer in Belgium Immobel, and the semi-public Belfius Insurance, launched a new NPO Up4North to bring the neighborhood to a 'turning point towards a dynamic, innovative area where different worlds meet, share and connect' (LabNorth, 2019). Moreover, they installed LabNorth, a consortium of creative agencies, to coordinate the experimental development of a new future for the neighborhood (LabNorth, 2019). As with the previous modes, dealing with uncertainty through urban planning cannot be thought outside of the economic regime and the uncertainties in which it is embedded. To uncover

this, the same questions essential to planning come to the fore: what and whose uncertainty about the future is dominant and how is this translated into the planning practice being introduced to deal with this uncertainty? Asking these questions, one main narrative is presented by the developers: 'Based upon the strengths of the area such as the good accessibility and the strategic location, they are all convinced that a major transformation is needed for the district' (LabNorth, 2019). Deconstructing this narrative, one can easily conclude that as one of the country's busiest train stations, multiple national and international bus services as well as metros and trams have been present for decades already, it does not explain the 'why now question.' Tellingly, the 'strategic' location, as similarly labeled by the region, is due to the vacancy rate in the area. As it increases to 20 per cent while multiple other buildings are planned and being built in the area, economic uncertainty is evident. After Fordism and flexible accumulation, this uncertainty is core to current financialization and coupled speculative accumulation dominating the current urban landscape. More specifically, the decoupling of use and exchange value holds a new economic uncertainty to generate rent gaps and find actors to sell or rent and monetize this gap (Smith, 1979).

This brings us to the core of today's experiments, which the WTC is part of. On the one hand, temporary use could serve as a real-world laboratory (Gieryn, 2006; Gross, 2016) to reintroduce new imaginaries in an area where lost memories of a different past and a nine-to-five present suck up all inspiration for the future. Next to a temporary exhibition, offices of various creative agencies, a pop-up swimming pool, as well as benches in front of the train station, the temporary use of the WTC most explicitly held the promise to serve this experimental purpose of temporary use. Multiple students and professors engaged with the neighborhood, iterating between a bird's-eye view and testing out interventions on the ground while rethinking an area that was long left unthought. While the propositions and models on the 24th floor did not look much different from those presented by Groupe Structures, the confrontation with the neighborhood's ground-level complexities brought important nuances that fed regular debates and elevator chats. These 'experiments' encompass 'new ways of doing things on a spatially and temporally bounded scale' (Caprotti & Cowley 2017: 1443) that 'couple intervention and observation' (Karvonen & van Heur, 2014; Karvonen, 2018) and are seen as a timely and promising antipode to modernist 'prediction and control' (Evans, 2011; Evans, 2016; Wohl, 2018), enabling actors to 'act despite vast uncertainties and gaps in knowledge' (Karvonen & van Heur, 2014b). This argument aligns with Badiou's (2012: 56) statement that 'a change of world is real when an inexistent of the world starts to exist in the same world with maximum intensity.' In that sense, this mode of planning is promoted as one that 'may provide some potential to challenge mainstream urbanization [and] propose radical visions for the future' (Hodson, Evans & Schliwa, 2018: 16).

On the other hand, this new practice seems to pacify criticism while rendering controllable the uncertainty rising from complex, fluid, and networked realities (Bulkeley et. al., 2018). Moreover, urban experiments seem to mutate and merge commonly experienced uncertainties with the risks of today's speculative accumulation (Harvey, 2014) in three ways. First of all, the boundedness of urban experiments could work both as an 'induced amnesia' for the horrors of the 2008 financial crisis as well as blinders for its role as a 'scout' or 'bait' to lower the 'risk' for a new round of speculative investment (Webb, 2018). This role of LabNorth and the various experiments in the area is not hard to imagine, as renters leave and developers prepare to reiterate a new *boom* after a strong *bust*. More precisely, it is distracting attention from the few who remember the €534 million of tax money and the promise of a 'public good' that is still bound to the ground on which the 'private' redevelopment of the area is taking place. Also, the experiments are generating a wave of uncritical newspaper articles and Instagram shots that are key to getting overseas investors on board.

Second, although these experiments are often praised for their 'change orientation' and 'place-based knowledge' by outside actors, they are barely taken seriously on the inside. In the Northern Quarter, and more specifically in the WTC, this is most visible in the blurred but factually different position of the different temporary users. Although the board in the elevator counts every temporary user as part of the lab, a contractual difference between them divides them into two major categories. The first holds a 'service contract,' allowing them to use the space for free in return for developing knowledge or, more specifically, a vision for the neighborhood. The second consists of most of the temporary users who all pay a reduced rent in return for engaging with the neighborhood. This clearly splits up the temporary users into the *scientists*, on the one hand, and the *lab rats*, on the other —with both the students and professors that temporarily used the WTC, despite their knowledge production activities, being part of the latter.

Third, in line with this blurry experimental setup, are the questions: *What are the hypotheses? What experiments can take place? Who is doing the monitoring? What factors are being looked at? When is an experiment defined as successful? How are lessons translated after and beyond the laboratory? What weight do these lessons have on the future of an urban project?* Without being transparent about what mechanisms are under the hood of experimental urban development, they become empty signifiers that are bound to fall prey to capture. Rather than testing hypotheses, these experiments would then minimize their role as testing hypotheses and serve as 'demonstrators.' Put differently, 'They are about context-revision, not sensitivity. They demonstrate adaptability and flexibility in the face of aspiration under conditions of heightened uncertainty. The particular elements brought together within a city demonstrate global aspiration that signals attraction and flexibility for capital accumulation' (May & Perry, 2016: 37). Although its deductive embracing of 'actual worlds'

Third, in line with this blurry experimental setup, are the questions: What are the hypotheses? What experiments can take place? Who is doing the monitoring? What factors are being looked at? When is an experiment defined as successful? How are lessons translated after and beyond the laboratory? What weight do these lessons have on the future of an urban project?

seems to answer the woes of inductive modernism and the urban traumas of Brussels and the Northern Quarter, it also falls prey to post-political critique as it forecloses debate (Swyngedouw, 2007; 2017) and discredits antagonism in service of consensus (Mouffe, 2005). As pointed out by May and Perry (2016: 38), 'We find apparent legitimacy for the adoption of a universal method that readily permits "scientism" to saturate the realm of political responsibility but also indicates willingness for the city to be a place of continual adaptation to the demands of neoliberal capitalism.' Although the experimental city narrative is actively associating itself with the 'radical,' the formalized laboratory setting for urban experiments indeed holds the power of defining 'the very parameters of what is considered "possible" in the existing constellation' (Žižek, 1999: 199 in Swyngedouw, 2007) and begs critical inquiry into the possibility to overcome it.

Building on the former arguments, a strong case could be made that experiments—and more specifically those taking place in the Northern Quarter of which the temporary use of the WTC is part— are a laboratory for 'urban governance rationalities' in the stretch of the financial crisis that 'reinforces the pre-crisis discursive construct of the city as a strategic site for the deepening and extension of neoliberalization' (Oosterlynck & Gonzalez, 2013: 1081). Put differently, 'if experimentalism is a strategy for urban transformation, it is an "affirmative" (Fraser, 2003) one which runs the risk of 'bolstering business-as-usual outside the experimental bubble, tinkering at the edges of a broken system' (May & Perry, 2016: 41). Although experiments indeed offer a promising new way of bridging process and environmental uncertainty via science, its contemporary economic capturing indeed refashions the means of urban production but seems to leave capital accumulation as its fundamental 'ends' untouched (Peck, Theodore & Brenner, 2010).

In this article, I have aimed to position the temporary use of Brussels's WTC in a broader temporal and spatial context of urban development. Its position in a context of urban experimentation through temporary use is de-isolated from and again embedded in a layered history of city-making. To do so, I used the lens of uncertainty as an underresearched but core element of planning, and urban planning more specifically. In doing so, I claim that through the economic conditioning of time and space, the social construction of uncertainty is influenced so that dominant experienced uncertainties in society are mutated to merge with economic uncertainties. As a consequence of this merger, acting upon these economic uncertainties through urban planning is legitimized as 'common good' while 'fixing' economic crisis tendencies and reproducing dominant power structures through the production of space (Lefebvre, [1974] 2008). By denaturalizing uncertainty as a social construct, the process of dealing with it through urban planning is politicized and planned futures decolonized (Giddens, 1999). In uncovering the process of urban experimentation and the position of the temporary use of the WTC therein, the questions of both whose uncertainty about the future is dominant in the planning process and how it is dealt with are treated. More specifically, by highlighting the various uncertainties between 'the actual' and 'the possible' (Badiou, 2012), I aim to recover the core political practice of 'foregrounding and naming different urban futures' (Swyngedouw, 2007: 71). Finally, by evacuating the merits of urban experimentation to do so, this contribution aims to repoliticize the power relations between *scientists* and *lab rats* in the experimental city.

REFERENCES

Abbott, J. (2005). 'Understanding and Managing the Unknown: The Nature of Uncertainty in Planning.' *Journal of Planning Education and Research*, 24(3), 237–251. https://doi.org/10.1177 /0739456X04267710.

Abbott, J. (2009). 'Planning for Complex Metropolitan Regions: A Better Future or a More Certain One?' *Journal of Planning Education and Research*, 28(4), 503–517. https:// doi.org/ 10.1177 /0739456X08330976.

Abbott, J. (2012). 'Planning as Managing Uncertainty: Making the 1996 Livable Region Strategic Plan for Greater Vancouver.' *Planning Practice and Research*, 27(5), 571–593. https://doi.org/10.1080 /02697459.2012.701788.

Badiou, A. (2012). *The Rebirth of History*. London; New York: Verso.

Beauregard, R. A. (1989). 'Between Modernity and Postmodernity: The Ambiguous Position of US Planning.' *Environment and Planning D: Society and Space*, 7(4), 381–395. https://doi.org/10.1068 /d070381.

Caprotti, F., & R. Cowley (2017). 'Interrogating Urban Experiments.' *Urban Geography*, 38(9), 1441–1450. https:// doi.org/10.1080/027236 38.2016.1265870.

Davies, G. (2010). 'Where Do Experiments End?' *Geoforum*, 41(5), 667–670. https://doi.org/10.1016 /j.geoforum.2010.05.003.

Evans, J. (2016). 'Trials and Tribulations: Problematizing the City through/as Urban Experimentation.' *Geography Compass*, 10(10), 429–443. https://doi .org/10.1111/gec3.12280.

Friend, J. K., & W. N. Jessop (1969). *Local Government and Strategic Choice: An Operational Research Approach to the Processes of Public Planning*. London: Tavistock Publications.

Gans, H. J. (1969). 'Planning for People, Not Buildings.' *Environment and Planning A: Economy and Space*, 1(1), 33–46. https://doi .org/10.1068/a010033.

Gross, M., & W. Krohn (2005). 'Society as Experiment: Sociological Foundations for a Self-Experimental Society.' *History of the Human Sciences*, 18(2), 63–86. https://doi.rg /10.11 77/0952695105 054182.

Harvey, D. (1989). 'From Managerialism to Entrepreneurialism: The Transformation in Urban Governance in Late Capitalism.' *Geografiska Annaler: Series B, Human Geography*, 71(1), 3–17. https://doi.org/10.1080 /04353684.1989. 11879583.

Healey, P. (2009). 'The Pragmatic Tradition in Planning Thought.' *Journal of Planning Education and Research*, 28(3), 277–292. https://doi.org/10.1177 /0739456X08325175.

Heathcott, J. (2005). '"The Whole City Is Our Laboratory": Harland Bartholomew and the Production of Urban Knowledge.' *Journal of Planning History*, 4(4), 322–355. https://doi.org/10 .1177/1538513205282131.

Hillier, J. (2013). 'On Relationality and Uncertainty.' *disP – The Planning Review*, 49(3), 32–39. https://doi.org /10.1080/02513625.2013 .859005.

Hodson, M., J. Evans & G. Schliwa (2018). 'Conditioning Experimentation: The Struggle for Place-Based Discretion in Shaping Urban Infrastructures.' *Environment and Planning C: Politics and Space*, 36(8), 1480–1498. https://doi.org/10.1177 /2399654418765480.

Karvonen, A., & B. van Heur (2014). 'Urban Laboratories: Experiments in Reworking Cities: Introduction.' *International Journal of Urban and Regional Research*, 38(2), 379–392. https://doi.org/10.1111 /14682427.12075.

Kenny, M., & J. Meadowcroft (eds.) (1999). *Planning Sustainability*. London; New York: Routledge.

Le Corbusier (1935). 'La Ville Radieuse' (The City Radiant with Joy). Speech on 'The Woman's Radio Review.' WEAF-NBC.

Marris, P. (1987). *Meaning and Action: Community Planning and Conceptions of Change*. 2nd rev. ed. London: Routledge & Kegan Paul.

Meadowcroft, J. (2009). 'What about the Politics? Sustainable Development, Transition Management, and Long Term Energy Transitions.' *Integrating Knowledge and Practice to Advance Human Dignity*, 42(4), 323–340. https://doi.org/10.1007 /s11077-009-9097-z.

Powell, R. C., & A. Vasudevan (2007). 'Geographies of Experiment.' *Environment and Planning A*, 39(8), 1790–1793.

Simone, A. (2013). 'Cities of Uncertainty: Jakarta, the Urban Majority, and Inventive Political Technologies.' *Theory, Culture & Society*, 30(7-8), 243–263. https:// doi.org/10.1177/02632 76413501872.

Thrift, N. (2004). 'Intensities of Feeling: Towards a Spatial Politics of Affect.' *Geografiska Annaler: Series B, Human Geography*, 86(1), 57–78. https://doi.org/10.1111/j .04353684.2004.00154.x.

Dieter Leyssen

On Gatekeepers and Moments of Translation

INTRODUCTION

In recent decades, both academia and policy have increasingly turned to cities and urban areas when discussing societal challenges. When confronted with global challenges such as climate change, migration, security, and a more fragile global economy, solutions are often sought in the urban context. City governments struggle to provide effective responses to these challenges. Transfers of competences from other government levels change the way cities are organized, especially when they do not come with a proportional increase in resources (Da Cruz, Rode & McQuarrie, 2019: 1). In various cities, reorganization comes with the establishment of interorganizational partnerships and public-private collaborations to secure sufficient resources. Urban policymakers turn to the development of networks to increase the chances of a policy outcome but also to lever resources and expertise beyond public funding (Blanco et al., 2011: 297). The effectiveness of these public-private partnerships is often questioned. Urban planners struggle to secure policy outcomes in a field increasingly defined by crises and scarcity. In this paper, I explore pathways for the planning discipline to provide more effective answers to the above challenges in this new context.

In the following sections, I question whether network-based urban planning can be effective in the implementation of urban policies, more specifically concerning matters of housing. I characterize network-based urban planning as a form of planning in which social networks between public, private, civic, and academic organizations are structural. In the literature on urban governance, the effectiveness and legitimacy of such network-based forms of governing are a recurring point of discussion (Rhodes, 1997; Blanco et al., 2011; Swyngedouw, 2005). Yet relatively limited empirical evidence exists to support theoretical claims (Da Cruz, Rode & McQuarrie, 2009). With this paper, I wish to contribute to this larger discussion by introducing two concepts: moments of translation and gatekeepers. These concepts provide the theoretical

framework by which to analyze a real-life case study of a context in which I have been involved since 2017. First, the paper provides an overview of the literature on networks and urban governance. Secondly, I present the theoretical framework for the case study, introducing the two main key concepts. The third section outlines the methodology used to gather and analyze the data. The fourth section presents the actual case study, in which the urban renewal process and the actors involved are mapped in time, space, and network. The conclusion lists my findings and highlights the relevance of this methodology for broader empirical and comparative analyses in the research on urban governance.

LITERATURE STUDY

In the past three decades, an abundance of literature has appeared on how the city is planned beyond the traditional elected government and official administrators (for extensive overviews, see Blanco et al., 2011; and Da Cruz, Rode & McQuarrie, 2019). In 1989, David Harvey insisted on shifting attention from 'government' to 'governance,' as the 'real power to reorganise urban life' did not lie in government but 'within a broader coalition of forces within which urban government and administration have only a facilitative and coordinating role to play' (6). First, I will introduce the network aspect in network-based urban planning, based on literature from network and policy theory. This will be followed by an overview of the more recent discussions on the efficacy and legitimacy of urban governance.

Network vs. Structural Analysis

An important contribution to the research of networks comes from a group of social anthropologists known as the Manchester School that emerged in the late 1960s. They reacted to structural functionalism in the social sciences. Structural functionalism emphasizes the social structure of society as a whole and the defined social function of its constituent elements. In this tradition, 'institutions and norms derived from internalized values of individuals' (Prell, 2012: 33). Based on field research in cities in Western Europe, India, and South Africa, the researchers of the Manchester School argued that interpersonal relations and their development into new structures and patterns could enable new group norms and new social institutions (Barnes, 1972; Bott, 1955; Mayer, 1961; Mayer, 1966; Mitchell, 1974). The researchers developed a theoretical and empirical base for a more 'empowering' field of research in which greater power is granted to the individual to shape his or her situation.

The Manchester School developed the basis for network analysis that is still used today. The network is operationalized by assigning characteristics to 'ties' (relations between people) or 'nodes and vertices' (the individual actors) that could be measured. They also explored the use of graphics representing networks and its characteristics that resonated in scientific, artistic, and popular contexts.

The effectiveness of these public-private partnerships is often questioned. Urban planners struggle to secure policy outcomes in a field increasingly defined by crises and scarcity.

Networks, Hierarchies, and Market

Another strand of literature is insightful for our understanding of networks in organization studies. Analyzing the economic institutions of capitalism, the economist Oliver E. Williamson (1985) distinguished markets and hierarchies as distinct modes of organization characterized by different types of relations. He explains that relations in a market organization are based on contracts and property rights and prices are the main means of communication. Actors are by default independent; collaborations only happen when there are incentives to do so, such as higher yields or lower costs. In hierarchical organizations, by contrast, an authoritative integrating structure is imposed, and communication happens through routines or bureaucracy (Lowndes and Skelcher, 1998: 318). In subsequent debates, Williamson's dyad of organizational types was complemented with a third pole: market, state, and community (Streek and Schmitter, 1985); price, authority, and trust (Bradach and Eccles, 1991); markets, politics, and solidarity (Mayntz, 1993); or markets, hierarchies, and networks (Thompson et al., 1991). While the former two organizational types were based on personal advantage or routine, the latter is based on trust, loyalty, and reciprocity. The basis for these relations is the joining of 'complementary strengths' of two actors and organizations (Lowndes and Skeltcher, 1998: 319). These three organizational types occur as hybrid forms. In many market-oriented contexts, relations are maintained and decisions are taken based on trust, while at the same time contractual relations are present in networks. These hybrid forms of organization, in which diverse sorts of relations are maintained, are ubiquitous in contemporary society, especially in cities.

Network-Based Governance and Urban Planning

Da Cruz, Rode, and McQuarrie (2019: 1) point out that the way cities are being organized is changing rapidly, as they struggle to provide effective responses to contemporary challenges. According to Harvey (1989: 6), the transition 'from managerialism to entrepreneurialism' or from 'government to governance' led to a process of deregulation and increased flexibility in planning processes, as well as an increased involvement of private-sector parties and a decrease in interest in public authority. An increase in the number of responsibilities that was often not met with a proportional budget increase led to 'more networked forms of governance, expanding the number and diversity of actors involved in an increasingly nonlinear policymaking process that challenges hierarchical integration' (Da Cruz, Rode & McQuarrie, 2019: 6). The characteristics of governance differ throughout the literature. Two trends can broadly be identified (Blanco et al., 2011). The first links governance directly to networked forms of organization. Rhodes (1997: 15) defines governance as 'self-organising, inter-organisational networks characterized by interdependence, resource exchange, rules of the game and significant autonomy of the state.' He considers governance as a shift from previous forms of organizing society. The second trend does not link governance to network-based ways of organization. They argue that governance can be characterized by hierarchies, the market, and networks. For them, governance has always existed but only recently received scholarly interest (Blanco et al., 2011). In this paper, I will use the latter interpretation of governance and add the prefix 'network-based' when appropriate.

Another discussion in literature concerns the efficacy and legitimacy of urban governance. Again, two strands can be identified. The first celebrates urban governance as a 'third way' that helps to overcome the rigidities of bureaucracies and the inequalities linked to the marketplace (Rhodes, 1997; Stoker, 2004, in Blanco, 2013: 277). They argue that networks allow, on the one hand, for a more effective mode of organization and, on the other hand, for a more inclusive one through mechanisms such as participation and public consultation. The second links network governance intimately to neoliberalism and presents a skeptical approach toward network-based governance (Brenner and Theodore, 2002; Swyngedouw, 2005). Swyngedouw (2005) argues that the introduction and legitimization of private and civic players in decision-making processes risks undermining political citizenship and the democratic process. While governance innovation could lead to more inclusive and effective decision-making, it likely will not in the current climate of erosion of the democratic character of the political sphere and the encroachment of market forces that define the 'rules of the game' (Swyngedouw, 2005: 1993). The problem, however, is the lack of empirical evidence to support both stances, notably on the city and local scale.

THEORETICAL FRAMEWORK

In this paper, I introduce two theoretical concepts I find useful for the analysis of network-based urban planning: moments of translation and gatekeepers. These concepts are borrowed from, respectively, science and technology studies and planning and network theory.

The Phases of a Process of Translation

In his study of a scientific experiment in a fishing village in the north of France, Michel Callon (1986) describes a process of translation. He distinguishes five moments in this process. First, there is the phase of problematization, in which an urgency renders certain actors indispensable within a network. In Callon's case study, he presents a shrinking catch of scallops in the bay and three researchers promoting a new technique to cultivate them. The next phase is called 'interessement,' during which an alliance is formed by representatives from different groups with aligned interests. So-called devices of interessement are used to shift these differing interests toward a single goal. Callon (1986: 72) explains: 'To interest other actors is to build devices which can be placed between them and all the other entities who want to define their identities differently.' The third phase, 'enrolment,' stands for the definition and coordination of roles among these representatives. 'Interessement' achieves 'enrolment' when successful. The fourth phase he discusses is 'mobilization,' when the shift of interest expands to other individuals linked to the representatives. As a fifth phase, Callon identifies 'controversy,' during which the representative's legitimacy is called into question and the alliances fall apart.

Gatekeepers and the Strengths of Weak Ties

Secondly, I propose to look at the concept of the gatekeeper. In his practical theory of urban planning, Pahl (1970: 267) discusses urban planners as 'gatekeepers' for public investment in the city. As intermediaries between state and local communities, they decided where public money got invested and where not. Simultaneously, they were the point of contact for demands from these communities. As such, they 'held the gate' between government and citizens and were regarded as important intermediaries for the transmission and reproduction of knowledge, consent, and trust. More recent case-study material on urban planning has shown that this role is increasingly taken up by actors related to the private or civic sector (Mayer, 2017; Forrest and Wissink, 2017; Baina and Landaub, 2018). Increasingly, gatekeepers are consultants working for government, private, or nongovernmental organizations, or community workers who do work 'in the field' and thereby make many connections and relations.

In 'The Strength of Weak Ties,' Granovetter (1973) argues that, for any intermediary, it is more important to have many indirect but weak links to contacts in a network rather than direct strong ones. These weak links will enable access to information and resources beyond your own circle. Based on a comparative case study in two working-class districts in Chicago, he found that the community characterized by strongly knit family ties proved to be less effective in defending their stakes in the urban renewal of their district than the community with high enrollment in employee associations and other organizations and characterized by more ties but weaker ones. Inside a network, gatekeepers tend to maintain many weak ties rather than a few strong ones.

METHODOLOGY

The paper looks at the urban renewal process of the Brussels Northern Quarter from 2015 to 2019. It engages with a real-life context and relies on multiple sources of evidence collected through observation, participation in meetings and workshops, structured and nonstructured interviews, and desk research on policy documents and secondary literature.

First, I examined the period from 2015 to 2019 making use of Callon's framework of translation. Based on an analysis of policy documents, the housing challenges and policies in Brussels are explained. Two in-depth interviews with key stakeholders in the district and a reading of secondary literature make it possible to distinguish the different stances of different groups in the district toward these policies. Based on these first explorations, I list eight organizations which I suspect could be characterized as gatekeepers in the district: public planning agency Perspective, Brussels Government Architect (BMA), private association Up4North, property owner Befimmo, architectural practice 51N4E, community organizations Harmonie and BRAVO, and activist Facebook page 'Which Way is North?' Structured interviews were conducted with all eight organizations. While all surveys were taken with individuals, they have been anonymized, and the name of the organization will be used. Based on the interview, a timeline is constructed and moments in which translation takes place identified. For each moment, the impact for the policy outcomes is described.

While the first part of the case study focuses on the when, the second part scrutinizes the who. Based on the survey, a limited social network analysis (SNA) is performed. Its scale remains limited because only eight organizations were surveyed, while an SNA normally entails an exhaustive mapping of an entire network. Therefore, we will focus mainly on the relations of those who were interviewed. The approach aims to visualize and discover the number and strengths of relations or ties between actors in a network in the urban renewal process of the Northern Quarter. It also reveals the extent to which actors operate as intermediaries or gatekeepers.

CASE STUDY

Juridically, the Brussels-North area is part of three different municipalities: the City of Brussels, Schaerbeek, and Saint-Josse. Situated next to the Brussels-North train station, the country's largest, it has historically been an arrival district for newcomers to the city. In the 1960s and 1970s, large parts of the station area were cleared to make place for the megalomaniac Manhattan Plan, a master plan comprising 70 office towers alongside the intersection of two highways. Due to consequent crises, the plan was only partially built and the cleared zone remained a wasteland, to the anger of displaced inhabitants and community organizations (for a more complete history, see Martens and Vanden Eede, 1994, and Doucet, 2017). Today, the business district is characterized by monofunctional office towers and broad boulevards. It is estimated that 35,000 people commute daily to the area (perspective.brussels, 2019: 49). Next to the business district, multiple social-housing projects were built to rehouse the evicted population. Today, this area, named Héliport-Anvers, is home to the majority of the district's inhabitants. The area received national attention as refugees squatted the local park during the refugee crisis of 2015. The third part of the district, Masui, dates from before the 1960s. It is an 'arrival city,' in which migrant communities typically find first opportunities for housing and work (perspective.brussels, 2019: 49).

Like many European cities, Brussels is struggling with a 'rise in property prices, the lack of housing accessible to low-income households, and the situations of inadequate housing experienced by more and more households' (Dessouroux, 2016: 1). A stark supply deficit is emerging in the segment of low-priced rental housing (Bauwelinckx et al., 2014). The local press frequently addresses the shortage of social housing (Bruzz, 2016; Knack, 2017), while analysts have pointed to the lack of rent control on the private market (Bernard, 2014). Another recurring point is the monofunctional office district with a high degree of vacancy, such as the Northern Quarter and the European administrative center. In light of the housing shortage, activist groups are claiming these spaces by squatting them for housing.

The citywide housing question is also present in the Northern Quarter. The Sustainable Regional Development Plan (PRDD) underlines a need for 'the establishment of housing' and 'the reintegration of an urban mix' in the district (perspective .brussels, 2019: 22, citing PRDD, 2013). The focus on a programmatic mix is also a priority for Up4North, an umbrella association bringing together nine large property owners in the district (BXL1, 2017). Articles written by representatives from civic organizations and community groups denounce the vacancy of office buildings, considering the housing shortage. Regarding a call for a programmatic mix, they question whether this will include 'housing [...] for residents likely to anchor in the neighbourhood and for less moneyed inhabitants?' (BRAL, 2009; 2019). In interviews with social workers in the district, two main challenges emerge regarding housing in the district. The first is the problem of the illegal subdivision of houses into smaller units, leading to overcrowding and poor living conditions. The second is the poor quality of existing social housing. The Héliport-Anvers part of the district counts 18.28 social dwellings per 100 families while the Brussels average is 7.7 (perspective.brussels, 2019: 50). Many of those are in need of renovation.

This overview reveals two policy questions regarding housing: (1) the shift to a programmatic mix including housing, and (2) the increase of affordable housing. In the analysis, we will focus on these two questions when looking for policy outcomes of the presented planning process.

Part 1
Timeline Analysis

From the conducted structured interviews, three large phases can be identified. All three are strings of events. These events did not happen in a linear sequence but in parallel, involving different stakeholders. The following overview explores whether the two presented policy outcomes were reached.

Phase 1: Problematization

In May 2015, a debate was held on '50 years of the Manhattan Plan' by a group of neighborhood organizations supported by academic and cultural associations. In 1965 the first high-rise, World Trade Center towers I and II, was built. The debate was organized by Maximiliaan Farm, a community farm in the west of the district, and the community center Harmonie. In remembrance of the clearing of the old district, movies and presentations on the district were shown. It was known at that time that WTC I and II were up for redevelopment. One of the social workers from Harmonie explained: 'During the debate [...], we talked a lot about the future and about the WTC. [...] Together with the social coordination [an association working on social cohesion in the Northern Quarter], we started a committee of inhabitants with the idea that the redevelopment of WTC is symbolic, so we need to do something.' She explained further that at the time, 'We [the different community organizations] signed a shared statement, demanding that the redevelopment of WTC incorporate new housing.'

The second event in this phase is the founding of the association Up4North by eight large property owners active in the Northern Quarter in November 2016. The ending of a series of large long-term lease contracts created a prospect of 30 per cent vacancy (Bogdan and Van Broeck, 2013). The move of 2,600 government administrators from the district to a nearby former logistic site converted into a mixed quarter was an eyeopener for private property owners (interview, perspective.brussels, 2019). The mission statement of Up4North declared that the association's goal was to 'group different stakeholders with an interest in the Northern Quarter [...] to develop a vision and implement a shared action plan and communication strategy, aiming to promote the district' (publication in *Belgian Official Gazette*, 2016). From 2017 onward, the board appointed two external project managers to elaborate and steer this action plan. According to various stakeholders interviewed, the foundation of Up4North was a pivotal step in the renewal of the district. An urban planner at the regional planning agency Perspective explains: 'They were the first to put the urgency on the agenda and mobilize different stakeholders.' Activist group 'Which Way is North?' emphasizes how Up4North was an important vehicle in 'lowering risks in the synchronic wave of

Dieter Leyssen

On Gatekeepers

reinvestment after disinvestment, knowing their [the property owners'] projects would be part of a larger shift of their context that would result in good prospects of profit' (interview, 'Which Way is North?,' 2019).

Both events react to different urgencies. The first denounces the lack and poor quality of affordable housing. The upcoming wave of urban renewal is seen as opportunity to solve this. The second is a reaction to the foreseen vacancy due to the end of lease contracts. It can be seen as the problematization in the process of translation.

Phase 2: Interessement

A second phase is a period stretching from June 2017 to September 2018. This phase is structured by two parallel strings of events.

The first is linked to an experimental project of temporal use of WTC I. This project was supported and realized by LabNorth. This loose association of architects, planners, and policy designers joined forces with Up4North to stimulate a 'citywide debate' on how to 'turn the district into an inclusive and attractive part of Brussels' (Lab North, 2018: 7). Through an open call, spaces were rented for low prices to associations and companies in the social, cultural, and creative sectors. One floor was turned into an atelier of the Faculty of Architecture of the University of Leuven, another was turned into a coworking space for the LabNorth association.

Thanks to the different projects organized during this period, such as workshops, events, and seminar weeks, various policymakers found their way to the building and the district. A public official from the Brussels Government Architect explains: 'A kind of buzz had arisen among many people who had joined juries and workshops. […] You just had to take the elevator. How was this possible? Normally there are only gray mice here, now the square meters are up for grabs' (interview, BMA, 2019). During this period, Perspective appointed an urban planner to look into the territory of the Northern Quarter. Perspective, BMA, and LabNorth jointly organized a symposium and workshop on the future of the district. Regarding housing, the report notes that 'the introduction of housing in the neighbourhood could have a positive impact on the neighbourhood because it would provide use all day around and not only during working hours' (perspective.brussels, 2019: 96).

The neighborhood's community organizations also recall the period of temporal use as a moment of exchange. A public program of exhibitions, lectures, workshops, and walks called *You Are Here* was set up by Architecture Workroom Brussels, one of the associations behind LabNorth. A social worker from BRAVO explains: 'During the exhibition, we organized a series of walks. I also contributed as a speaker. It was a space for discussion and dialogue' (interview, BRAVO, 2019). For a social worker of Harmonie, the walks were first and foremost a way to gain information on the projects in the Manhattan part of the district (interview, Harmonie, 2019). Feelings regarding their involvement are ambiguous. On the one hand, they were interested and willing to collaborate. On the other, it was not clear to them whether or how their input would be considered. One social worker relates that at a certain moment 'we were solicited a lot to participate in projects, to mobilize people, but at a certain point we stopped doing so. We had the feeling that we were being abused. We did look for people to participate, but in the end completely different projects came out, actually not for the neighborhood's benefit' (interview, Harmonie, 2019).

A second string of events concerned the plans for the redevelopment of the WTC I and II buildings. After previously failing to find new tenants, the property owner had turned to the Brussels Government Architect with the question of co-organizing an architecture competition. The newly assigned team of architects, urbanists, and engineers would have to prepare a proposal to attract a program of 70,000 m^2 for the Flemish Government. Two preconditions attached to this competition are relevant for this inquiry. First, the Flemish Government was asking specifically for a mixed-use building. Secondly, the Brussels Government Architect demanded to include housing. They explain: 'My hypothesis is that homes should be included in the Northern Quarter. I am guessing that the market is ready, with the current housing prices in Brussels and the strategic location of the neighborhood, to absorb relatively cheap pioneer homes. This is a hypothesis that I repeat in different environments, until someone bites and wants to develop a test case' (interview, BMA, 2017). A team of architects was appointed, including 51N4E. The project was developed in a studio that was part of the temporal use. Owners, architects, engineers, and advisers met on a daily basis in the on-site atelier to evaluate the design and programmatic choices. The BMA advisory board regularly passed by.

One social worker relates that at a certain moment 'we were solicited a lot to participate in projects, to mobilize people, but at a certain point we stopped doing so. We had the feeling that we were being abused. We did look for people to participate, but in the end completely different projects came out, actually not for the neighborhood's benefit'

Befimmo's project coordinator relates: 'The way of working was new for everyone. We had never done a project like that. You got to know each other much better, since you simply spend more time together' (interview, Befimmo, 2019). The appointed team of architects provided a plan that convinced Befimmo, the BMA, and the Flemish Government.

Coined 'the zebra,' a spatial concept was developed in which office and residential floors alternate. Housing was integrated alongside a hotel, sports facilities, and a large greenhouse on the ground floor. However, the housing would not be subsidized. According to the project coordinator of Befimmo, the economic model of the project did not allow for 'low rents and subsidized units' (interview, Befimmo, 2019).

At this moment, different parties involved in the district—the public authorities, community organizations, owners, and planners—were collaborating and interacting in various ways. This corresponds with the phase of interessement. Two 'devices for interessement' can be distinguished, positioned between different actors to shift interests toward a single goal. The first is the WTC I as a vacant container for temporal uses. This created the first alignments of property owners, policymakers, and a creative community using the tower as office or atelier space. However, it did not stimulate full interest of the local community organizations. The second device for interessement is the zebra scheme proposed by the architects. The combination of both devices meant that the first policy outcome regarding a programmatic mix including housing was successfully translated to a broader group. However, the phase did not result in a guaranteed integration of affordable housing.

Phase 3: Controversy

In December 2018, the WTC I tower was vacated in preparation for the upcoming redevelopment. While there was still a lot of vacant space in the district, it proved impossible to negotiate new temporal office spaces for all temporal tenants. In the end, only 9 out of 46 organizations found a new space in the area. In the same period, LabNorth failed to formalize its association. Some of its members remained present in the district but in a more scattered form. Across all interviews, these events are seen as negative for the further urban renewal of the district. Up4North's project manager confirms that 'the move from WTC I harmed the coalition of actors. The disintegration of temporary use also halted projects that were planned' (interview, Up4North, 2019).

In March 2019, the design for the WTC was published publicly under the name 'ZIN.' The final design includes 69 per cent office space (of which 4 per cent co-working space), 13 per cent housing, and 15 per cent hotel facilities. Different reactions can be distinguished. The community organizations expressed mixed feelings. One of the social workers explains: 'As far as I know, only a very small percentage in the project will be social housing, if any at all. The housing aspect in ZIN does not

at all address the current needs of the district' (interview, BRAVO, 2019). In the framework of the public consultation organized by the municipal authority, 'Which Way is North?,' a Facebook page sharing news and opinions on the urban renewal of the district, collected all questions and remarks on the project proposal from community organizations and academic actors. Two topics emerge from the questions and demands. The first addresses the lack of 'social mix' as opposed to the programmatic mix proposed in the project: the project does not address the district's needs in terms of housing or employment ('Which Way is North?,' 2019). The second addresses the transparency of the procedure: the public consultation is highly bureaucratic and too short. In the public debate, however, ZIN was received positively: 'When I saw the ZIN project, I was quite happy that the principles that we had been talking about were actually translated in the project. Because it's one thing to talk about things, but something else to actually do it' (interview, perspective.brussels, 2019). According to one of the policymakers, 'It tests new types of functional mix, of inhabiting the ground floors and of reaching out to different initiatives. It addresses the owner's needs, but also the needs of the neighborhood' (interview, perspective.brussels, 2019).

In this phase, the representativity of certain actors is called into doubt. The early outcomes of the translation process cause controversy: while a success to some, the redevelopment of WTC I and II failed to convince all the stakeholders involved. Another reason for this controversy lies in the clash between the network-based, hierarchical organizations. An example is the failing of LabNorth to further develop their activities in a context characterized by hierarchy and the market.

Part 2
Social Network Analysis

The second part of the analysis focuses on the actors and the ties between them. While the previous part investigated the phases of urban renewal in the Northern Quarter, this part provides a snapshot of the network of organization in July 2019. The eight organizations interviewed constitute the starting point of this mapping.

We are interested in measures that indicate whether an organization performs as a gatekeeper. A first such measure is the distribution of ties over five categories: public, private, civic, academic, and media. Up4North has the widest distribution. Perspective and 'Which Way is North?' are second and third. For Perspective and 'Which Way is North?,' the highest concentration of ties lies in their own category, respectively public and civic, while for the private association Up4North, the highest concentration lies with public organizations.

For each tie identified, the strength was estimated. Up4North and 'Which Way is North?' have on average strong links overall. Perspective.brussels has rather strong links to private organizations, while BRAVO mainly has strong links to public entities. Referring to Granovetter's 'strength of weak links,' we can suggest that Up4North, with many ties and a wide dispersal over different categories, and an average strength of ties, appears again as an important intermediary in the network.

We now shift focus from the eight organizations interviewed to the entire network. First, we analyze the centrality of the organizations. Centrality can be defined by (1) the 'degree centrality,' including all outgoing and incoming ties of one unit, (2) the in-degree centrality, including only the ties for which the organization is on the receiving end, and (3) the out-degree centrality, including only outgoing ties.

Evidently, two groups can be distinguished: those who were interviewed and those who were not. In the group interviewed, Up4North shows the most links, followed by perspective.brussels and the Brussels Government Architect. Among the organizations that were not interviewed, Architecture Workroom Brussels, the Municipality of Brussels, and both academic institutions, KU Leuven and Vrije Universiteit Brussel, had the most ties. The measure of in-degree centrality shows the 'trustworthiness' of organizations in the network. The most referred-to organizations are perspective.brussels, Up4North, Architecture Workroom Brussels, and the Municipality of Brussels, followed by the BMA and the two academic institutions, KU Leuven and VUB. The measure of out-degree centrality lies in the same line of centrality, with Up4North having the most links, followed by perspective.brussels, the Brussels Government Architect, and Harmonie.

A third measure we applied is 'betweenness centrality.' In our network, the organizations occupying such a position are Up4North, followed by Harmonie and 'Which Way is North?' This means that these organizations serve as 'bridges' between other, unconnected organizations. This result suggests that Up4North and Harmonie are the two most important 'gatekeepers' in the network.

The last step in our limited social network analysis is the identification of clusters. Three clusters can be identified. The first includes 24 organizations that were strongly linked to the temporal use of WTC I. They include the organizations behind LabNorth, as well as perspective.brussels and the BMA and the organizations involved in the ZIN project. Up4North is the most central organization of the respective cluster. A second cluster includes the community organizations based in Masui and Héliport-Anvers. In this cluster, Harmonie is the most central node. A third cluster comprises a series of more recent organizations with an activist position, the main organization being 'Which Way is North?' Again, these clusters can be analyzed in their diversity of the organizations they contain.

Based on these different measurements, we can identify three important gatekeepers in the network: Up4North, Harmonie, and 'Which Way is North?' Up4North can be characterized as a gatekeeper because of its number of relations, their average strength, and the diversity of related actors. Harmonie and 'Which Way is North?' have, according to the limited survey, fewer ties which are relatively stronger and more oriented toward peers from the same sector.

This conclusion supports Swyngedouw's claim that urban governance beyond the state does not equal a more empowering or more democratic form of urbanism; on the contrary, it could consolidate the power of economic and institutional elites. This could be avoided if other gatekeepers, from the civic and activist realms, were given sufficient capacity to work 'in the network' and advocate their respective policy agendas

CONCLUSION

What can we learn from both analyses regarding policy outcomes in networked-based urban planning? Based on a single case, it is impossible to draw conclusions regarding policy outcomes from the investigated process that can be generalized. Nevertheless, we can highlight some emerging trends that need further research.

Legitimacy and the Risk for Monopolization of the Network

The limited social network analysis identified private association Up4North, community organization Harmonie, and activist Facebook page 'Which Way is North?' as gatekeepers in the network. Up4North advocated policy outcomes regarding the programmatic mix, the latter two advocated outcomes regarding affordability. To date, outcomes regarding the programmatic mix are being translated, while outcomes regarding affordability are not. The analysis also proved Up4North to be a more important gatekeeper than the other two organizations. This should not be surprising, as the goal of the organization, as stated in their founding statement, is to support partners and create a shared vision for the district. As such, their daily activities and projects are meant to support network-based urban planning. For Harmonie, the activities linked to the urban planning of the district come on top of their daily work, which is to support local inhabitants and the elderly. 'Which Way is North?,' by contrast, focuses on research and creating a critical attitude toward the urban-planning process. Our results suggest a monopolization of the network by one actor that pushes selectively those policies that meet its agenda. This conclusion supports Swyngedouw's claim that urban governance beyond the state does not equal a more empowering or more democratic form of urbanism; on the contrary, it could consolidate the power of economic and institutional elites. This could be avoided if other gatekeepers, from the civic and activist realms, were given sufficient capacity to work 'in the network' and advocate their respective policy agendas. Further research should be done on how gatekeepers coming from different realms can work together and, in doing so, increase the legitimacy of network-based urban planning.

Efficacy and the Use of Spatial Design as Devices of Translation

Given the high diversity of actors, each with their own professional language, translation was suspected to be of great importance. Four 'moments of translation' were identified. Those that were successful in reaching policy outcomes were the temporal use of WTC I and the ZIN project. In both processes, the device for translation was spatial. In the first, it was the vacant WTC I building serving as a container for experimental uses. In the second, it was the 'zebra' scheme integrating housing and office space in one building. This suggests the potential of spatial aspects, explored through design or experimental use, for the effectiveness of network-based urban planning. More research can highlight the possibilities and pitfalls of spatial design as a translating device among actors from different fields.

Further empirical research should be done on other cases to create broader evidence for the hypothesis of the paper. This paper contributes to discussions on the theoretical and analytical frameworks to look at network-based forms of governance. By highlighting the importance of moments of translation and gatekeepers, as well as the risk of monopolization, I hope to stimulate researchers and practitioners in urban planning to evaluate their role and feel empowered when entering the arena of urban redevelopment projects.

REFERENCES

Adaba, G., & D. Ayoung (2017). 'The Development of a Mobile Money Service: An Exploratory Actor-Network Study.' *Information Technology for Development*, 23(4), 668–686.

Bain, A., & F. Landau (2018). 'Artist Intermediaries in Berlin: Cultural Intermediation as an Interscalar Strategy of Self-Organizational Survival.' *Urban Research & Practice*, 11(3), 247–262.

Barnes, J. A. (1969). 'Graph Theory and Social Networks: A Technical Comment on Connectedness and Connectivity.' *Sociology* 3(2), 5–32.

Barnes, J. A. (1972). *Social Networks*. Modular Publ. Anthropol. 26. Reading, Mass.: Addison-Wesley.

Bauwelinckx, A., I. Bensaïd, L. Chemin, C. Dumont & W. Van Mieghem (2014). 'Produire des logements sociaux aujourd'hui et demain. Partie 1: Le foncier/ Les finances.' *Rassemblement Bruxellois pour le Droit à l'Habitat*, no. 58.

Bernard, N. (2014). 'Encadrement des loyers (grille "de reference" et taxation des loyers réels) et déductions fiscales des intérêts des emprunts hypothécaires ("bonus logement"): Développements récents.' In: N. Bernard (ed.), *Vers un encadrement des loyers? La défédéralisation du bail d'habitation: Quel(s) levier(s) pour les Régions?* Brussels: Larcier, 287–325.

Blanco, I. (2013). 'Analysing Urban Governance Networks: Bringing Regime Theory Back In.' *Environment and Planning C: Government and Policy*, 31(2), 276–291.

Blanco, I., V. Lowndes & L. Pratchett (2011). 'Policy Networks and Governance Networks: Towards Greater Conceptual Clarity.' *Political Studies Review*, 9(3), 297–308.

Bogdan&VanBroeck and Idea Consult (2013). 'Ferraris.' Unpublished study for the Flemish Government.

Bott, E. (1957). *Family and Social Network*. London: Tavistock.

Bradach, J., & Robert G. Eccles (1992). 'The Organization and Management of Chains: Owning, Franchising, and the Plural Form.' ProQuest Dissertations and Theses.

Brenner, N., & N. Theodore (2002). *Spaces of Neoliberalism: Urban Restructuring in North America and Western Europe*. Malden, Mass.; Oxford: Blackwell.

Callon, M. (2017). 'Some Elements of a Sociology of Translation: Domestication of the Scallops and the Fishermen of Saint-Brieuc Bay.' *Logos* (Russian Federation), 27(2), 49–94.

Carayannis, E., T. Barth & D. Campbell (2012). 'The Quintuple Helix Innovation Model: Global Warming as a Challenge and Driver for Innovation.'

Journal of Innovation and Entrepreneurship, 1(1), 1–12.

Cubitt, T. (1973). 'Network Density among Urban Families. In: J. Boissevain, J. C. Mitchell (eds.) (1973). *Network Analysis: Studies in Human Interaction*. The Hague: Mouton.

Da Cruz, N., P. Rode & M. McQuarrie (2019). 'New Urban Governance: A Review of Current Themes and Future Priorities.' *Journal of Urban Affairs*, 41(1), 1–19.

Davies, J. (2014). 'Coercive Cities: Reflections on the Dark Side of Urban Power in the 21st Century.' *Journal of Urban Affairs*, 36(s2), 590–599.

Dessouroux, C., R. Bensliman, N. Bernard, S. De Laet, F. Demonty, P. Marissal, & J. Surkyn (2016). 'Housing in Brussels: Diagnosis and Challenges.' BSI Synopsis. *Brussels Studies*.

Doucet, I. (2015). *The Practice Turn in Architecture: Brussels after 1968*. New York: Ashgate.

Forrest, R. (2017). 'Whose City Now? Urban Managerialism Reconsidered (Again).' *Sociological Review*, 65(2), 155–168.

Granovetter, M. (1973). 'The Strength of Weak Ties.' *American Journal of Sociology*, 78(6), 1360–1380.

Hamilton, M. (2011). 'Unruly Practices: What a Sociology of Translations Can Offer to Educational Policy Analysis.' *Educational Philosophy and Theory*, 43(1), 55–76.

Harvey, D. (1989). 'From Managerialism to Entrepreneurialism: The Transformation in Urban Governance in Late Capitalism.' *Geografiska Annaler: Series B, Human Geography*, 71(1), 3–17.

Lowndes, V., & C. Skelcher (1998). 'The Dynamics of Multi-organizational Partnerships: An Analysis of Changing Modes of Governance.' *Public Administration*, 76(2), 313–333.

Madden, David J., & Peter Marcuse (2016). *In Defense of Housing: The Politics of Crisis*. London: Verso.

Marin, B., & R. Mayntz (1991). *Policy Networks: Empirical Evidence and Theoretical Considerations*. Frankfurt am Main; Boulder, Colo.: Westview Press.

Martens A. & M. Vanden Eede (1994). *De Noordwijk: Slopen en wonen*. Berchem: EPO.

Mayer, A. C. (1966). 'The Significance of Quasi-Groups in the Study of Complex Societies.' in: M. Banton (1966). *The Social Anthropology of Complex Societies*. London: Tavistock.

Mayer, M. (2017). 'Whose City? From Ray Pahl's Critique of the Keynesian City to the Contestations around Neoliberal Urbanism.' *Sociological Review*, 65(2), 168–183.

Mayer, P. (1961). *Tribesmen or Townsmen: Conservatism and the Process of Urbanization in a South African City*. Cape Town: Oxford Univ. Press.

Mayntz, R. (1993). 'Governing Failures and the Problems of Governability: Some Comments on a Theoretical Paradigm.' In: J. Kooiman (ed.) (1993). *Modern Governance*. London: Sage.

Mitchell, J. (1974). 'Social Networks.' *Annual Review of Anthropology*, 3(1), 279–299.

Pahl, R. E. (1975). *Whose City? And Further Essays on Urban Society*. Harmondsworth: Penguin.

Prell, C. (2012). *Social Network Analysis: History, Theory & Methodology*. London: Sage.

Rhodes, R. (1997). *Understanding Governance: Policy Networks, Governance, Reflexivity and Accountability*. Buckingham: Open University Press.

Rode, P. (2019). 'Urban Planning and Transport Policy Integration: The Role of Governance Hierarchies and Networks in London and Berlin.' *Journal of Urban Affairs*, 41(1), 39–63.

Rolnik, R. (2019). *Urban Warfare: Housing under the Empire of Finance*. London: Verso.

Schaeffer, S. (2007). 'Graph Clustering.' *Computer Science Review*, 1(1), 27–64.

Scotti, I., & D. Minervini (2017). 'Performative Connections: Translating Sustainable Energy Transition by Local Communities.' *Innovation: The European Journal of Social Science Research*, 30(3), 350–364.

Stoker, G. (2004). *Transforming Local Governance: From Thatcherism to New Labour*. New York: Palgrave Macmillan.

Streek, W., & P. Schmitter (eds.) (1985). *Private Interest Government*. London: Sage.

Swyngedouw, E. (2005). 'Governance Innovation and the Citizen: The Janus Face of Governance-beyond-the-State.' *Urban Studies*, 42(11), 1991–2006.

Thompson, G., J. Frances, R. Levacic & J. Mitchell (eds.) (1991). *Markets, Hierarchies and Networks: The Coordination of Social Life*. London: Sage.

Thompson, G., C. Pforr & Curtin University of Technology School of Management (2005). *Policy Networks and Good Governance: A Discussion*. Perth: School of Management, Curtin University of Technology.

Tonkiss, F. (2013). 'Austerity Urbanism and the Makeshift City.' *City*, 17(3), 312–324.

Williamson, O. (1985). *The Economic Institutions of Capitalism*. New York: Free Press.

Internet Sources:

Arikan, B. (2016). 'Analysing Data Networks.' Available at: https://blog.graphcommons.com/analyzing-data-networks/ (accessed 15 August 2019).

Befimmo (2019). 'Befimmo haalt overheidsopdracht Vlaamse Overheid binnen.' Available at: https://www.befimmo.be/sites/default/files/imce/publications/befimmo_nv_-_zin_-_nl_-_12_03_2019_embargo_17u40_-_final.pdf (accessed 12 May 2019).

Boie, G. (2018). 'Welcome in Jaspers Town.' Available at: https://a-plus.be/actuel/welcome-in-jasperstown/#.XVU2wugzbD4 (accessed 12 May 2019).

BRAL (2012). 'Noordwijk: De geschiedenis herhaalt zich?' Available at: https://bral.brussels/en/artikel/noordwijk-de-geschiedenis-herhaalt-zich (Accessed 12 May 2019).

BRAL (2018). 'Mais que se passe-t-il au quartier Nord?' Available at: https://bral.brussels/en/artikel/mais-que-se-passe-t-il-au-quartier-nord (accessed 12 May 2019).

Degreef, C. (2009). 'Woonruimte ligt voor het oprapen in Brussel.' Available at: https://www.bruzz.be/politiek/woonruimte-ligtvoor-het-oprapen-brussel-2009-05-06 (accessed 12 May 2019).

Delbeke, K. (2017). 'Bouwen, cashen, slopen.' Available at: https://www.standaard.be/cnt/dmf20170616_02928477 (accessed 12 May 2019).

Knack (2019). 'Betaalbaar en duurzaam wonen.' Available at: https://www.knack.be/nieuws/belgie/betaalbaar-en-duurzaamwonen-brussel-heeft-noodaan-een-groot-renovatieplan/article-opinion-1259283.html (accessed 15 July 2019).

Lemaire, P. (2018). 'Noordwijk. Nieuwe perspectieven.' Available at: https://a-plus.be/focus/ herstructurering-van-denoordwijk/ (accessed 12 May 2019).

Van Garsse, S. (2011). 'Balans van 45 jaar Noordwijk.' Available at: https://www.bruzz.be/samenleving/balans-van-45-jaarnoordwijk-2011-04-01 (accessed 12 May 2019).

'Which Way is North?' (2019). 'WTC I & II to ZIN_ Questions & Comments.' Available at: https://www.facebook.com/pg/whichwayisnorthbxl/notes/ (accessed 12 May 2019).

Policy Documents:

Bruxelles participation (2017). *Inforum Quartier Nord*. 14/05. Available at: https://www.bruxelles.be/forums-de-quartier (accessed 12 May 2019).

Lahy, S. (ed.) (2016b). *Milieueffectenrapport van het ontwerp van Gewestelijk Plan voor Duurzame Ontwikkeling*. Brussels: Kabinet van de minister-president van het Brussels Hoofdstedelijk Gewest, 777 p. Available at: http://www.prdd.brussels/sites/default/files/prdd_rie_fr_web.pdf.

Perspective.brussels (2019). *Welke toekomst voor de noordwijk? Voortgangsverslag*. Retrieved via perspective.brussels.

Perspective.brussels, Brussels Bouwmeester & LabNorth (2018). 'North District: Next Steps?'

Nico Vandenplas, Sotiria Kornaropoulou, Diego Luna Quintanilla, and Gianmarco Causi, 'Habitat North: Strengthening the Ecological Potential through Alliance Projects,' https://labnorth.network/portfolio/habitatnorth/, last consulted: 28 April 2021.

'When we talk about habitat, we are talking about inclusiveness, which not only refers to flora and fauna, but also to social and spatial conditions. We can even think of a framework consisting of different degrees of inclusiveness, taking into account ecological, social and spatial systems. It is therefore essential to integrate and combine social practices, participation and co-creation processes with local organizations and residents. This makes it possible to find a meeting point between bottom-up initiatives and top-down organizations.'

Reconverting the Northern Quarter

A Discussion with Bahareh Sabouri, Sven Lenaerts, Caro Baens, Petra Pferdmenges, Marie-Anaïs Bluteau, Dieter Leyssen, and Mathilde Jacobs

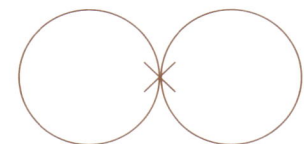

Moderated by Pierre Lemaire

Interview published in *A+270 Adaptive Re-Use* (February–March 2018) with Sven Lenaerts, coordinator of Up4North (NPO founded by the main real-estate operators in the NQ), who, together with Marie-Anaïs Bluteau (project manager at Vraiment Vraiment), Dieter Leyssen (architect at 51N4E), and Roeland Dudal (partner at AWB), set up the LabNorth open reflection network.[1] Also participating was Dr. Petra Pferdmenges, founder of Alive architecture and teacher in the BRU.S.L.XL studio at KU Leuven, where the academic agency Living North originated and of which her students Mathilde Jacobs, Caro Baens, and Bahareh Sabouri are members.[2]

[INTRO]   Today, the Northern Quarter (NQ) is at a tipping point. The expiry of leases for several large tenants and high vacancy rates have prompted the private and academic communities to roll up their sleeves and take up the challenge. The public sector is ready to follow suit. *A+* reports on these multiple initiatives.

PL   Pierre Lemaire
BS   Bahareh Sabouri
SL   Sven Lenaerts
CB   Caro Baens
PP   Petra Pferdmenges
MAB   Marie-Anaïs Bluteau
DL   Dieter Leyssen
MJ   Mathilde Jacobs

PL   It seems clear that the NQ is undergoing a transformation. In your opinion, is the decline of the neighborhood attributable to the intrinsic characteristics of the Manhattan Plan?

BS   What is immediately obvious is the neighborhood's monofunctional office vocation and the important place given to the car in the public space. This leads to a certain monotony in terms of form and use of the public space. It is also apparent that the district is divided into three relatively contrasting zones: the administrative section with its office towers; a portion mainly devoted to social housing and school buildings; and finally, the area along the canal where a number of high-end housing projects are currently under development. These areas are physically separated by wide boulevards, and their respective populations do not intersect. Furthermore, the poor quality of public spaces in terms of use does not encourage people to stay there, let alone visit the area.

SL   Many people see the Manhattan Plan as an example of what is wrong in terms of urban planning. This negative connotation affects the attractiveness of the area. In terms of physical experience, the presence of many blind plinths and urban barriers does not help. Most of the office buildings are well over twenty years old and are unsuited to today's working environment. Together with the lack of services in the broadest sense of the word, this is probably the main reason why many businesses are choosing to leave the area.

On the other hand, the NQ has tremendous potential. In addition to its very large inventory of available office space and its strategic location near the city center, it is hyper-accessible thanks to the presence of the multimodal hub of the station, but also the canal and the inner ring road. Combined with the upward trend in the vacancy rate (10–15 per cent), this observation suggests that we need to rethink the typical office building model.

Our challenge today consists in rethinking the model by integrating the principle of multi-occupancy and the vertical mix of housing and offices. With new office occupancy models and a new service offer, the tenants will return.

It might be interesting to develop an 'inclusive gentrification' attitude whereby we seek to build socio-economic dynamics between the various actors according to their needs and competencies. Already, the field studies and contacts made by the students of the BRU.S.L.XL studio have had an impact on everyday life. Gradually, they are becoming the mediators of the ongoing transformation.

1. Unfortunately, Roeland Dudal was not present during the interview.
2. The BRU.S.L.XL studio at KU Leuven was founded in 2015 by Petra Pferdmenges, Nele Stragiers, and Christopher Paesbrugghe to conduct design research from 1:1 (S) to neighbourhood scale (XL) in visions for Brussels.

PL   In a sense, you are looking for new followers of the NQ that, together with the current inhabitants and users, can revive the NQ. Who are the audiences you meet today in the NQ?

CB   From 9 a.m. to 5 p.m. you have the employees and civil servants, and after 5 p.m. you have the residents for whom there are very few services available—no supermarket, no café. To complete the picture, the Parc Maximilien has attracted a new public, immigrants. And finally, there are the property owners themselves.

PP   It might be interesting to develop an 'inclusive gentrification' attitude whereby we seek to build socioeconomic dynamics between the various actors according to their needs and competencies.
Already, the field studies and contacts made by the students of the BRU.S.L.XL studio have had an impact on everyday life. Gradually, they are becoming the mediators of the ongoing transformation.

PL   Were you able to identify entry points where to focus your efforts in this vast project in a context of fragile public finances?

MAB   We put forward methods for initiating the project by bringing together all the publics. This was done through workshops aimed at discussing what was feasible, what was desired … To pool ideas and to try and overcome apparent contradictions between stakeholders. Although the viewpoints of the inhabitants, landlords, and employees may have initially appeared contradictory, the workshops led to the emergence of a common desire for a more pleasant neighborhood.
The project extends to the creation of the Platform North website, whose inclusiveness we consider essential. Beyond the local community, we want to spread the buzz to the rest of Brussels.

DL   The experimentation we initiated here was partly inspired by the fact that the authorities lacked a long-term vision or master plan. A number of stakeholders thus decided to take matters into their own hands. From an originally private initiative, the project was subsequently adopted by civil society and then by the academic world. This led to an abundance of ideas and studies that would probably not have been possible in a traditional urban study. For example, Petra, Nele, and Christopher's BRU.S.L.XL studio is excellent at bridging the gap between architectural and urban visions, on the one hand, and the actual activation of the neighborhood through interventions on the ground, on the other. In the studio that Freek and I run, we focus on the classic arteries of the district and more particularly on how to make the Boulevard Simon Bolivar the dominant artery of the district rather than the Boulevard du Roi Albert II. I feel that our multilayered approach will outperform the results of a more traditional study.

PL Pierre Lemaire
SL Sven Lenaerts
PP Petra Pferdmenges
DL Dieter Leyssen
MJ Mathilde Jacobs

PL   In the redevelopment of the quarter, one of the major issues is that of urban intensity, or rather its absence. Did you tackle the issue of the activity of the urban fabric in your work?

MJ   Last week we opened the Café North for a day where we welcomed a diverse public: office workers, schoolchildren, etc. This is a typical ground-floor activation intervention that represents our ambition for the interaction between buildings and public space. This principle of services at the foot of buildings opened to all publics rather than just its occupants should indeed drive the way in which new buildings are designed.

PP   This example shows how important it is for students to incorporate the economic factor into their work if we want to go beyond an academic, idealistic vision. Synergies still need to be identified, particularly with Up4North. The purpose of creating the Living North academic practice within KU Leuven is precisely to break down the barriers between academics and professionals. It is also designed to pursue its work beyond the end of the studies.

DL   I think there are precedents for the question of interdependence between actors in urban projects. I am working on this issue as part of the LSE Cities international center. In many instances of temporary occupation or bottom-up processes, there is no real interdependence between owners and temporary occupants. Whereas in the case of ground floors, we could build up a genuine interdependence between stakeholders, whereby financial benefits would be shared. For example, we could imagine an economic loop where, in the common interest, the owners invest to support the temporary use of ground floors since it has a positive impact on the social capital of the neighborhood.

SL   In our work, to open up ground floors to services for the public, we are often confronted with new work patterns that all too often advocate the internalization of a whole range of services for their employees. As a consequence, employees do not leave their workplaces during the day. Therefore, our challenge is to dare to change this mentality by developing an innovative service offer that extends beyond those offered in office buildings.
In the European Quarter, for example, we have seen an evolution of housing typologies from studios to two-bedroom families over the last ten years. This is coupled with the opening of shops in the evenings and at weekends. This kind of virtuous circle could well be achieved in the NQ with the construction of housing along the major roads.

DL   One of the first hypotheses that we developed in LabNorth is the transition from 100 per cent single occupancy in the office buildings to 30 per cent multi-occupancy, sharing services on the ground floor. In any case, this is going to be done gradually over time.

PP   I believe that the conditions for the success of this project must involve using what is available rather than trying to reinvent the system. This is true in terms of space, society, and economy. We will only succeed in reinforcing the identity of the district if we integrate these three dimensions into our approach: the social—the users, their expertise, and their needs; the spatial—what is available and how to transform it; the economic—where the money is and how to develop alternative financing mechanisms.

PL   How do you envision the future of your work? A collaboration with the IABR 2018–2020?

SL   There are in fact plans to collaborate via the AWB agency, which is the curator of this edition. 'Urbanity' workshops will be held in the NQ and there are plans to organize a major cultural event in the NQ with all the cultural actors.

DL   I think indeed that the summer of 2018 will be a pivotal moment to discuss our relatively organic initiative work with several target audiences. This will be the occasion to hear from urban policy players and the suggestions they may have for an urban planning toolkit that incorporates the conclusions of our work. We could then also assess the qualities and points to be improved in this new type of workplace with the users of the multi-occupancy buildings. Finally, it would be interesting to have an exchange with the café architects on the design of flexible, or even evolving, buildings. In short, when the context is as rich and diverse as LabNorth, it is crucial to produce results that can be shared with as many people as possible.

Dieter Leyssen, Frederik Serroen, Freek Persyn, Heleen Verheyden, Kristiaan Borret, Pierre Lemaire, Roberto Bonaiuti, and Roeland Dudal, 'North District, Next Step?,' https://perspective.brussels/sites/default/files/poles/north_district_next_step_brochure.pdf, last consulted: 22 April 2021.

'Instead of projecting once more a utopian vision on this central part of the city, we must ask collectively: which direction do we take? Which defects should be solved, and which qualities strengthened? What kind of district does Brussels need and for who?'

Alessandro Gess

Alessandro Gess is an architect and urban planner, partner at l'AUC architects and urbanists in Paris. A graduate of the École Nationale Supérieure d'Architecture de Versailles (ENSAV) and of the Technical University of Munich (TUM), he holds an executive master's from Sciences Po Paris (Territorial Governance and Urban Development).

Amar Lalvani

Amar Lalvani is CEO of Standard International (the parent company of Standard Hotels) and Bunkhouse Group. Previously he led the global development of W Hotels. Amar has an MBA from Harvard Business School and a BS from the Wharton School of the University of Pennsylvania. In addition to serving on the boards of Standard International and Bunkhouse Group, he was a founding investor and board member of Peloton Interactive. He resides in New York City with his two daughters.

Bahareh Sabouri

Bahareh Sabouri is an architect. She obtained her master's in architecture from KU Leuven Ghent. Since 2020 she has been working at the multidisciplinary architecture office Maarten Dobbelaere, mainly focusing on renovation, restoration, and repurposing assignments. She is one of the co-founders of Living North, a project developed in the context of her training at KU Leuven.

Bernard Dubois

Attentive to contemporary codes, the Belgian architect Bernard Dubois designs sensitive spaces. Better, he blurs the lines between genres and, free from conventional architecture, allows them to live in context. In each project, surfaces meet and explain themselves: classic, modernist, post-modernist. Dubois draws inspiration from the different trends to create a coherence, to bring together what the history of architecture opposes. Whatever the nature of the project, the vocation of Dubois's architecture is to be informed, contextual, and fundamentally cultural.
Dubois graduated from La Cambre in 2009 and represented Belgium at the Venice Biennale in 2014. Next to his practice he is also co-director of the AA Visiting School Brussels since 2016.

Dieter Leyssen

Dieter Leyssen is an architect and urban sociologist. He holds a master's in architecture from KU Leuven and one in city design and social sciences from LSE. Since 2019 he has been a partner in the Brussels-based international practice 51N4E, where he is responsible for projects in civic design and adaptive infrastructure. He currently teaches at KU Leuven and Hasselt University.

Djamel Klouche

Djamel Klouche is an architect, urban planner, and co-founder of AUC architects and urban planners in Paris. A professor at the École Nationale Supérieure d'Architecture de Versailles, he is a laureate of the international consultation launched by the President of France on the Grand Paris in 2008, the Grand Pari(s). Along with Caroline Poulin and François Decoster, he was awarded the Grand prix de l'urbanisme 2021 by the Ministry of Ecological Transition.

Freek Persyn

Freek Persyn graduated from the Sint-Lucas School of Architecture in Brussels, having followed one academic year in Ireland at the Dublin Institute of Technology. Soon after obtaining his degree, and in parallel to working for Xaveer De Geyter architects, he co-founded 51N4E in Brussels. His trajectory has spanned a wide range of investigations, that besides architectural work include territorial plannning, strategies, and research. Today, besides co-managing the office, he is focused on cross-referencing between projects and programs. Since January 2019, in parallel to his professional activities at 51N4E, he is a professor of Architecture and Urban Transformation at the ETH in Zurich, holding a chair called Newrope.

Jan Denoo

Jan Denoo is an urban-agogue based in Brussels. He designs and guides urban transitions as a partner at the worker co-op Endeavour. He also initiates critical urban dialogues as a co-founder and curator of Stadsform, a center for dialogue about the city of tomorrow.

Johan Anrys

Johan Anrys graduated from the Sint-Lucas School of Architecture in Brussels, after one academic year in Ireland at the University College Dublin. Soon after obtaining his degree, he co-founded 51N4E in Brussels. He has been invaluable in establishing the quality of 51N4E's built work and has succesfully developed 51N4E's architectural practice in Tirana. Today, besides co-managing the office, he is responsible for the development of the programs of Metropolitan Hybrids and Transformative Densification. In parallel to his professional activities at 51N4E, he acts on a regular basis as a lecturer and as an expert for policymakers and industries.

John Eyers

John Eyers studied Architecture at LUCA School of Arts in Brussels. After graduating in 1984, he started working for the architectural firm Jaspers & Partners. At the age of 31 he founded his own practice, which merged with Jaspers in 2001. Today, Jaspers-Eyers Architects is one of the largest and most thriving architectural practices in Belgium, with offices in Brussels, Leuven, and Hasselt. The company is directed by John Eyers and his business partner Jean-Michel Jaspers.

Karine Dana

An architect by training, Karine Dana works as a journalist and videographer. Called upon for this dual skill and her architectural sensitivity, she collaborates regularly with international offices (among others, 51N4E, Lacaton & Vassal, and YTAA) in the context of competitions, research, and exhibitions. In 2017 Dana launched the subARCHITECTURE channel on Vimeo: https://vimeo.com/channels/1254948.

Koenraad Van Cleempoel

Koenraad Van Cleempoel is an art historian lecturing on architectural history and theory at Hasselt University. His current interest is the built-up meaning of heritage sites and the relation with new architectural interventions. With Bie Plevoets he co-authored *Adaptive Reuse of the Built Heritage* (Routledge). Previously he was the holder of the PP Rubens Chair at the University of California, Berkeley.

Kristiaan Borret

Kristiaan Borret has been the Bouwmeester Maître Architecte (BMA) of the Brussels-Capital Region since 2015. The BMA is an independent government official who stimulates and supervises the quality of urban development projects. He previously held the same position for the city of Antwerp. In 2017 he was appointed by the City of Amsterdam as quality supervisor for two urban transformation areas in Amsterdam. Borret has been a professor of urban design at Ghent University since 2005.

Marie-Anaïs Bluteau

Marie-Anaïs Bluteau is a graduate of the Nantes Atlantique School of Design. She heads the Brussels branch of the design agency Vraiment Vraiment. Through her first projects in Amsterdam and Berlin, she developed expertise in the area of the 'commons' through projects led directly by communities of users, such as the LabNorth initiatives in the Northern Quarter of Brussels and the Hangar du Kanaal in the Biestebroeck district.

Between urban design and service design, Bluteau now pays a great deal of attention to the animation of collective dynamics in order to draw innovative ideas from them. Prototyping and building positive, sustainable, and accessible environments together is at the heart of her concerns. For her, designing solutions also means bringing users together and rekindling enthusiasm around a subject.

Mathilde Jacobs

Mathilde Jacobs is an architect who graduated from KU Leuven Faculty of Architecture Campus Sint-Lucas Brussels. She is one of the founders of Living North, developed within the context of her training at KU Leuven. She works as a project architect at B-bis architecten, where she is responsible for smaller-scaled architectural projects, residential and public interior design, and scenographies for exhibitions and performing arts. She is also a co-founder of Collective, an architectural office that focuses on interior and renovation projects within an urban context.

Petra Pferdmenges

Dr. Petra Pferdmenges explores, through practice, research, and teaching, the role of the architect in inclusive city-making, with a focus on Brussels. She founded the Brussels-based spatial agency Alive Architecture in 2010 after having practiced for five years in internationally recognized architecture offices in Paris and Barcelona. In 2015 she completed her PhD in arts at RMIT Melbourne.

Pierre Lemaire

Pierre Lemaire is an architect and urban planner. After graduating from ISA St-Luc Tournai in 1996, he continued his studies of large-scale projects at the Architectural Association in London and the Bauhaus Kolleg in Dessau. He developed many master plans in the agencies KPF, ZHA, and Liebeskind. He has been working for ADT and perspective.brussels since 2010.

Roeland Dudal

Roeland Dudal is a founding member and director of Architecture Workroom Brussels, a cultural platform for innovation in the field of architecture and urbanism. He studied architecture at Ghent University. He is a guest professor for architectural design at the KU Leuven Faculty of Architecture in Ghent and Brussels.

Roxane Le Grelle

Roxane Le Grelle is an architect and art historian. After having worked for the magazine *A+ Architecture in Belgium* as programming coordinator for four years, she is now in charge of Culture and Public Interaction within 51N4E. In 2018 she co-curated the Belgian pavilion at the Venice Biennale of Architecture. In 2020 she co-founded Architecture Curating Practice, a platform that aims to develop architecture as a cultural practice by editing publications and curating exhibitions, among other things. More recently she started the position of curator at Archizoom, EPF Lausanne.

Sven Lenaerts

With a master's in marketing management and political and social science, Sven Lenaerts started his professional career in 2000 within the IT sector. Intrigued by the topic of cities and their future, he started working in 2013 in the domain of urban development as the manager of several associations in the Brussels-Capital Region aiming to revitalize districts by applying innovative governance and placemaking models. In 2021 he joined Immobel as Head of Corporate Social Responsibility.

Werner Joris

Over the past three decades, Werner Joris has acquired extensive experience in the Belgian real-estate scene. Working for some of the country's leading development firms and investors like CDP, IRET Development, and Befimmo, he has built a solid track record in large-scale project development as well as a deeply rooted affinity for the Brussels Northern Quarter and its revitalization.

In recent years he has been on the vanguard of a transition toward a more integrated and mixed-use perspective on real-estate projects. In continuation of this durable and contextual approach, he is now partner at Downtown Real Estate, a Brussels-based firm specializing in sustainable redevelopment and urban regeneration.

HOW TO PRODUCE CHANGE?

A CADAVRE EXQUIS FOR A NEW PROCESS OF TRANSFORMATION

Concept and Editing
Dieter Leyssen
Freek Persyn
Alessandro Gess
Roxane Le Grelle

Publication Team
Roxane Le Grelle
Alessandro Cugola

Texts by
Freek Persyn
Djamel Klouche
Koenraad Van Cleempoel
Dieter Leyssen
Karine Dana
Alessandro Gess
Roxane Le Grelle
Roeland Dudal
Jan Denoo
Pierre Lemaire

With
Kristiaan Borret
Werner Joris
Johan Anrys
John Eyers
Amar Lalvani
Bernard Dubois
Bahareh Sabouri
Sven Lenaerts
Caro Baens
Petra Pferdmenges
Marie-Anaïs Bluteau
Mathilde Jacobs

Quotes
Francesco Garutti
Jan de Moffarts
Dieter Leyssen
Frederik Serroen
Freek Persyn
Heleen Verheyden
Kristiaan Borret
Pierre Lemaire
Roberto Bonaiuti
Roeland Dudal
Isabelle Doucet
Almut Fuhr
Mathieu Berger
Louise Carlier
Nico Vandenplas
Sotiria Kornaropoulou
Diego Luna Quintanilla
Gianmarco Causi

Diagrams
Alessandro Cugola

Graphic Design
Studio Otamendi
(Manuela Dechamps
Otamendi assisted
by Yann Linguinou)

Copyediting
Patrick Lennon

Proofreading
Max Bach

Printing
Snel, Vottem - www.snel.be

Typeface
Akzidenz Grotesk BQ

Paper
Balance Silk 80 g.

Image credits
p. 4 © Johan Anrys
p. 63 © Alexis Gicart

Ruby Press
Schönholzer Str. 13–14
10115 Berlin
Germany
www.ruby-press.com

ISBN 978-3-944074-41-2

North Beach: turning the roundabout of Boulevard du Roi Albert II and Boulevard Simon Bolivar into an accessible pool for one day. Temporary intervention organized by Pool Is Cool, June 2018.

	From WTC to ZIN by Freek Persyn, November 2021	Coincidences by Djamel Klouche, May 2021	Rereading WTC by Koenraad Van Cleempoel, June 2019	Kristiaan Borret interviewed by Dieter Leyssen, November 2018	Filming Chance by Karine Dana December 2020	Challenging Real Estate by Alessandro Gess July 2021	Which Role for the Architect? A Discussion with Johan Anrys and John Eyers Moderated by Roxane Le Grelle, July 2021	Amar Lalvani and Bernard Dubois interviewed by Alessandro Gess, March 2021	Werner Joris interviewed by Alessadro Gess, January 2019	The Glass Trojan Horse by Roeland Dudal, June 2019	On Scientists and Lab Rats in the Experimental City by Jan Denoo, August 2019	On Gatekeepers and Moments of Translation by Dieter Leyssen, August 2019	Reconverting the Northern Quarter A Discussion with Bahareh Sabouri, Sven Lenaerts, Caro Baens, Petra Pferdmenges, Marie-Anaïs Bluteau, Dieter Leyssen, and Mathilde Jacobs Moderated by Pierre Lemaire, February 2019
DEAL WITH THE TRAUMA	X		X	X	X						X		X
CONFRONT AND LEARN	X			X	X		X			X	X	X	X
START WITH THE STRUCTURE	X	X			X	X	X	X	X				
COMMIT TO CIRCULARITY	X				X	X							
CARE AND CURATE	X	X			X			X				X	X
	[p. 4]	[p. 8]	[p. 11]	[p. 16]	[p. 23]	[p. 24]	[p. 26]	[p. 30]	[p. 34]	[p. 38]	[p. 41]	[p. 46]	[p. 56]